MILLING IN THE LATHE

MILLING IN THE LATHE

BY

EDGAR T. WESTBURY

MODEL & ALLIED PUBLICATIONS LIMITED
13/35 Bridge Street, Hemel Hempstead,
Hertfordshire, England

Model and Allied Publications Limited
Book Division, Station Road, Kings Langley,
Hertfordshire, England

© Model & Allied Publications Ltd. 1948

Second Edition 1948

Second Impression 1951

Third Impression 1960

Fourth Impression 1967

Fifth Impression 1970

Sixth Impression 1972

Seventh Impression 1973

ISBN 0 85344 101 4

Made and printed in Great Britain by Unwin Brothers Ltd., Old Woking, Surrey
for Model Aeronautical Press Ltd.

CONTENTS

PAGE

FOREWORD vii

CHAPTER I.—INTRODUCTION 1

Adaptability of the lathe for milling—Pros and Cons—
Evolution of milling processes—Classification.

CHAPTER II.—MILLING CUTTERS 7

Types of cutters—Number of teeth—Cutter grinding—
Single-point cutters—Principles of multi-point cutters
—Home-made cutters—Chucking end mills—Backing-off
cutters—Slitting saws—Woodruffe key-seating cutters.

CHAPTER III.—MILLING WITHOUT SPECIAL APPLIANCES 22

Use of normal lathe movements—Milling flat surfaces—
End milling—typical operations—Methods of fixing—
Setting up—Fluting connecting rods—Keyway milling
—Recessed valve chests—Side milling cylinder ports—
Screw heading—Fluting taps and reamers

CHAPTER IV.—THE VERTICAL SLIDE 55

Advantages of vertical adjustment—Elevating cross-slides
—Types of vertical slides—" Robbing Peter to pay
Paul "—Attaching work to vertical slide—Port cutting
—End fluting and slotting—Checking accuracy—Squaring
and levelling.

CHAPTER V.—ROTARY-SPINDLE ATTACHMENTS ... 75

Convenience for certain operations—Simple cutter frames
—Milling and drilling spindles—The Potts milling appliances—Vertical-column attachments—Milling spindle
arrangements—Grinding spindles—Cam generating—
Vertical milling attachments—Stencil milling—Two-
dimensional and three-dimensional copying—Planetary
milling.

CHAPTER VI.—MEANS OF DRIVING CUTTER-SPINDLES ... 100

Hand drive—Belt drive—Overhead gear—Construction of overhead gear—Flexible shaft drive—Motorised drive.

CHAPTER VII.—INDEXING GEAR 122

The divided headstock—Worm dividing appliances—Accuracy of dividing gear—Making division plates—The " Westbury " dividing attachment—The " Quickset " attachment—The " Eureka " attachment—The " Myford " attachment.

CHAPTER VIII.—APPLICATION OF LATHE MILLING PROCESSES 143

Advantages in model engineering—Milling small components—Fork joints—Crossheads—Axleboxes—Fluted columns—Ornamental turning methods—Feeds and speeds.

FOREWORD

OF the many ways in which the lathe can be pressed into service to perform operations outside the range of plain turning, few are more useful or more widely exploited than that of using it as a simple form of milling machine. Most model and experimental engineers, instrument makers and horologists, whose machine-shop equipment is limited, have at some time or other had recourse to methods of milling in the lathe. Yet the subject is one on which comparatively little practical information is available, and many text-books on the lathe omit any reference to it whatever.

Among the popular series of cheap *Model Engineer* handbooks published many years ago was one entitled *Milling in Small Lathes*, an elementary but thoroughly practical introduction to the subject, which has proved its usefulness in hundreds of workshops. Since this book has gone out of print, many lathe users have clamoured for its re-publication; but in view of the many developments in lathe milling processes, and new appliances introduced in recent years, there was a call for a more up-to-date and comprehensive work, embodying the results of much practical experience by the readers and staff of *The Model Engineer*.

The present book, therefore, while definitely based on the older and smaller handbook, may be regarded as an entirely new publication, in which the various methods of milling in the lathe are classified, and a very wide range of milling appliances described in detail. While no claim is made that it covers all possibilities, in respect of either apparatus or method, it should at least enable the practical worker to exploit, in many new and possibly hitherto unheard of ways, the utility of simple and limited workshop equipment, and make the lathe live up to its reputation of "the universal machine tool."

CHAPTER I

INTRODUCTION

THE adaptability of the engineers' lathe is recognised by all intelligent users, and it is probably the most versatile of all machine tools, though in modern production engineering its duties tend to become more and more highly specialised as new machine tools for specific purposes are evolved. In a machine shop which is organised for the manufacture of a definite class of product, it is usually profitable to use a variety of machines, each specially designed to carry out a limited range of operations with the utmost efficiency, and thus versatility becomes a very dubious, or even a negative virtue. But in the machine shop which needs to be capable of tackling any class of work encountered, particularly where the number or variety of machine tools is limited, the ability to adapt any machine to purposes other than that to which it was primarily designed is a most important practical asset.

It is not only in the model engineer's workshop that there is scope for using the lathe as a milling machine ; the instrument maker and horologist find it equally useful in this capacity, as may be proved by the fact that all well-known makers of instrument and watch lathes have listed a range of attachments for milling in the lathe ; and these, so far from becoming obsolete in modern practice, tend, if anything, to become more popular and varied.

Although equipment of this nature is less frequently provided for larger lathes, it is none the less applicable, and can often be used with advantage in the repair shop or garage

—unless the latter establishment is concerned merely with routine overhauling and the fitting of ready-made " spare parts."

Pros and Cons

It should not be necessary to defend or justify the practice of milling in the lathe ; though there is a good deal of controversy as to whether it is practical or worth while, there are few experienced operators who will question this point. One sometimes hears it said " The lathe is too limited in its movements for use as a milling machine," or " Small lathes are not rigid enough " ; other critics will compromise by saying " All right for a little fiddling job, but no use at all for production work." These objections must be taken into account in considering just what one may expect to be able to accomplish ; it is only by recognising the limitations of any tool or process that one can hope to use it to advantage.

Let it first be clearly understood that there is no question of a lathe competing on equal terms, in respect of either range or efficiency, with a well-designed milling machine for this class of work ; its main claim to consideration is its ability to fulfil, more or less efficiently, the duties of a milling machine when one is not available. But this does not mean to say that it should be regarded as simply a makeshift.

Much useful milling work can be done on the lathe, by the use of its normal movements and adjustments, but when, as often happens, these impose inconvenient limitations, they can be supplemented by the addition of attachments, such as a vertical slide or indexing head, which increase its scope. It is, however, important to note that the fitting of elaborate attachments to a lathe may not only make it cumbersome to manipulate, but also tend to increase troubles due to lack of rigidity, which is, perhaps, the most serious practical limitation, at least in the case of small lathes, when adapted to milling. The simplest rig which provides the required range of movements will generally be found to be the most efficient.

With regard to the ability of the lathe to tackle production milling, the question arises : What is production milling ?

If one takes it to mean the removal of large quantities of metal, as in slab milling and similar processes, the lathe is obviously unsuited to this work ; but there are many operations which are quite legitimately within the category of production work —such as screw slotting, tap and reamer fluting, keyway cutting, and so on, which can be carried out just as quickly on a lathe as on a milling machine ; indeed, in some cases, time can be saved by avoiding the need for re-setting work. We have heard a good deal in recent years about the hold-ups caused by " bottle-necks " in production work, and in the

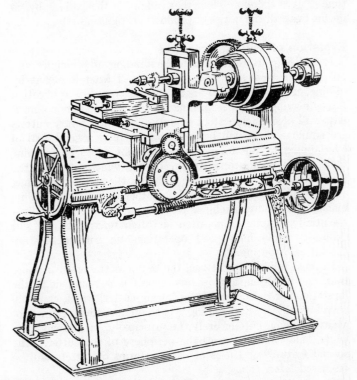

Fig. I. An early " Lincoln " type milling machine, the design of which shows many traces of its evolution from the lathe

writer's experience, these have often been caused by the lack of sufficient milling machines to handle quite small operations, which have often proved to be capable of being carried out in simple lathes which were standing idle. The greatest difficulty in such cases has been to get production engineers to realise these possibilities, as many of them have simply never heard of using a machine for anything outside its specific job.

A writer in *Machinery*, describing a fixture for carrying out a tricky milling operation, stated " the fixture was designed to fit on a lathe, as no milling machines were available at the time." It is therefore clear that milling in the lathe is by no means beneath the notice of production engineers.

Evolution of Milling Processes

It will help us to a clear understanding of principles and processes if we first have a clear idea of what is meant by milling, and then go on to review the progress of its application to engineering practice. Milling may be said to define almost any kind of a machine tool operation in which rotary cutters are employed. It will be seen that there is a good deal of overlapping in the functions of different types of machine tools, as, for instance, in rotary boring, which is within the legitimate scope of either the lathe or the milling machine, and in drilling, which can be done either in the lathe, milling machine, or drilling machine. Keyway cutting with end mills— essentially a milling operation—is often referred to as " slot drilling," while high-speed operations on soft metals are classed as " routing."

In most milling operations, the cutter is traversed in more than one direction, and in this respect is not subject to the limitations of the plain drill or boring cutter, which can only travel axially. " End milling " is characterised by the use of a cutter which cuts entirely, or principally, on its end face, while " side milling " uses the periphery of the cutter. The special features and uses of various forms of cutters will be discussed later.

It is quite possible that milling processes were first evolved in conjunction with lathe work, and Holtzapffel and other early writers on machine tools show many applications of rotary cutters on the lathe.

The horologists were probably the first to evolve a machine specifically intended for milling, to cope with the necessity for some means of cutting the teeth of clock gears quickly and accurately. Cutters having a large number of fine teeth were employed at first, and this type of cutter still persists for some classes of work.

In the first milling machines employed in engineering practice, the relationship to the lathe is at once recognisable. The " Lincoln " type milling machine, introduced about 100 years ago, consisted of a lathe bed on which was mounted a more or less normal type of slide-rest and a headstock, also somewhat similar to that of a lathe, except that it was provided with means of raising and lowering the mandrel. This general form of machine, improved in detail, is still used for certain purposes, but the " knee and column " type of machine, which gives a far greater latitude of vertical adjustment, is by far the more popular, and is made in a wide variety of types for horizontal, vertical and adjustable-angle milling.

A consideration of the various types of modern milling machines, and the methods by which they are applied, is by no means beside the point in a treatise on lathe milling processes, as it helps one to understand the underlying principles of these processes and gives one ideas on how to use them to best advantage.

Classification of Milling Processes

It has already been mentioned that the lathe cannot be recommended for carrying out heavy milling operations which involve the removal of large masses of material at a high rate of output. Beyond this, however, nearly all known milling operations can be carried out in the lathe, even including the more complicated operations, such as gear cutting, spiral milling profiling, and form generating, which are often considered to be the exclusive province of the elaborate universal milling machine. The scope of milling in the lathe, so far as variety of work is concerned, is limited only by the ingenuity of the operator and the pains which he is prepared to take in fitting up fixtures and attachments, and in setting up the work.

In reviewing processes, typical examples of each, taken not only from the writer's personal experience, but also that of contributors to *The Model Engineer* (to whom due acknowledgment will be made), the main object is to demonstrate, by concrete examples, the methods of tackling various problems which arise in normal model engineering practice. Of the innumerable types of milling appliances which have been described in *The Model Engineer*, at various time, only representative examples, or those embodying especially interesting features of design, will be illustrated. Reference will also be made to proprietary milling appliances which have been produced by makers of lathes or their accessories.

CHAPTER II

MILLING CUTTERS

ALTHOUGH there is no essential difference between the milling cutters used on a machine specially designed for this class of work and those used for milling in the lathe, it is proposed to consider the subject of cutters primarily from the latter aspect and, in particular, to show how the lathe user can make the most of a very limited variety and number of cutters, or even produce simple forms of cutters which will serve his purposes as efficiently as those of the ready-made type. The forms of cutters which are designed particularly for heavy work, or for the rapid removal of metal at high rates of feed, speed and power, are of but little interest to the lathe user, because, as we have seen, neither the power nor the rigidity of the ordinary lathe is adequate to do justice to them ; but on the other hand, true cutting efficiency, in the sense of carrying out work rapidly with the minimum expenditure of power, is of the utmost importance for lathe milling, and it is quite impossible to produce either accurate or well-finished work with inefficient cutters.

One of the arguments often raised against any form of milling operation is that it entails the use of expensive cutting tools, and that a wide variety of such tools is necessary to cover a normal range of operations. This objection certainly applies in cases where cutters must be bought, and where the special cutter for a particular operation is insisted upon ; but it is not necessarily true if one is prepared to exercise a little ingenuity, or even plain common sense, in the adaptation

7

of available cutters, or the construction of cutters to suit emergency requirements.

Types of Milling Cutters

It is possible to class nearly all forms of milling cutters under three general headings : (1) Those with radially projecting teeth, designed to cut on the periphery only ; (2) those with endwise (axially) projecting teeth, which cut on the end face only ; and (3) those which combine forms (1) and (2) so that they can be used in either capacity, or in which the teeth are set at an intermediate angle for bevel cutting. Class 1 includes cylindrical milling cutters for plane milling of flat surfaces, also narrow disc cutters for slotting or keyway cutting, and practically all varieties of form cutters, such as those used for cutting gear teeth and similar profiles (Fig. 2). Class 2 comprises the very wide variety of cutters known as " end mills " or " slot drills," and when of large diameter, these are termed " face mills," or " shell end mills," the latter term being generally applied to a short, hollow cutter designed to be mounted on an arbor (Fig. 3). Class 3 is perhaps the most versatile class of all, including " side and face " cutters which can be used for either peripheral or end face cutting, or for tee slotting, dovetail cutting, and the formation of vee slides, angular grooves, etc. (Fig. 4). Most modern end mills are provided with side cutting teeth, though their efficiency to cut in this direction is limited, and generally speaking, only the tips of the side teeth are used. It should, however, be pointed out that no end mill could work at all, except in the capacity of a spot facing cutter or counterbore, without some ability to take a shallow side cut. These observations on cutter design are elementary, but may help us to understand the principles involved in the various milling operations.

Number of Teeth

Milling cutters may have any number of teeth, from one upwards, the single-toothed type of cutter being generally known as a " fly-cutter." This type has obvious limitations in cutting efficiency, since the rate at which it can remove

Fig. 2. Slotting cutter and convex form cutter

Fig. 3. Shell end-mill

Fig. 4. Bevel cutter and vee-angle cutter

metal is restricted, and in most cases it is only in contact with the work for a brief part of a revolution ; moreover, the load fluctuation caused by intermittent cutting may set up serious vibration or " chattering." Nevertheless, the simple fly-cutter should not be despised, as it is the simplest of all cutters to make or adapt, and it is applicable to many problems, especially in form milling, which would otherwise require an elaborate and expensive special cutter. In cases where the rate of removing material is not the prime consideration, single-point cutters are useful, even in production work.

It is logical to expect that increasing the number of teeth in a cutter will improve its cutting efficiency, since each of the teeth is capable of contributing to the work ; but the idea that the cutter having the largest number of teeth will be the most efficient is a fallacy. Some of the first milling cutters used had very fine-cut teeth, being practically rotary files, but it was soon found that a smaller number of teeth gave better results. In the first place, a difficulty arises in keeping a large number of teeth in proper cutting condition; it is also necessary to provide proper chip clearance between the teeth, so that the cutters do not become clogged ; and it is also found that taking fairly deep bites with a cutter having few teeth is better than taking a mere scrape with a fine-tooth cutter, absorbing less power and producing less heating or general wear and tear.

The exact number of teeth most suitable for a milling cutter depends to a great extent on its size, speed, and general conditions of duty. Most cutters give their best results when each tooth is removing the amount of metal best suited to its rake and clearance angles—just as a drill has a " natural " rate of cut at which it works most comfortably and lasts longest.

It is logical that small, high-speed cutters, especially those used on soft metals, should work best with few teeth, whereas larger and slower cutters may utilise a larger number of teeth with advantage. Within the class of work dealt with here, it is rarely advisable to use a cutter having more than about twelve teeth. The importance of running cutters of any kind dead truly will be appreciated, because it is only in this way that each tooth can be made to contribute its full quota of work. A cutter running very badly out of truth may, in fact, only be cutting on one tooth ; and in that case, it would only be functioning as a fly-cutter, and a rather inefficient one at that.

Cutter Grinding

One of the difficulties which the amateur or small shop operator encounters with milling cutters is the problem of grinding them properly. It should be emphasised that this can only be carried out by means of a grinding machine equipped with means of indexing the cutter teeth and grinding them all exactly alike. Suitable attachments to an ordinary tool-grinder may serve this purpose, but attempts to sharpen the cutters without such aids are almost inevitably futile, and generally result in spoiling them completely. It is, however, practicable to touch up the teeth of a cutter which is only slightly dull by the use of a fine carborundum or oil-stone slip.

Single-point Cutters

An ordinary lathe boring-bar, designed to run between centres or in the chuck, can be adapted to carry a single straight cutter for peripheral milling, or an angular, offset or bent tool which will act as a " side and face " cutter. Generally speaking, however, the scope of a bar of this type is rather limited, unless it is designed in the first place to cover this particular class of work, which often involves the use of cutters of greater length and heavier section than those employed for boring. The form of holder generally used to take fly-cutters on milling machines, as supplied by several of the leading makers, is as shown in Fig. 5. It will be seen that the shank is heavy to promote rigidity, tapered to fit the milling machine spindle, and equipped with a draw-in bolt (not shown) to secure it in position. Note that the cutter is fitted so that its edge falls on the diametral centre line, in order to simplify the measurement of rake and clearance angles of the cutter. Examples of form cutters suitable for use in a holder of this type are shown in Fig. 6.

The simple cutter holder shown in Fig. 7 has been referred to in *The Model Engineer* several times in the past, and is one of the handiest, both to fit and apply to work, in the small lathe. By fitting the cutter at an angle of about 45 deg. to the axis, it can be used for both side and face work, and various shapes of tools points may be used.

Some forms of tool holders used in normal lathe practice can be adapted to carry rotary fly-cutter bits by mounting them in the lathe chuck, or on the faceplate, so that the cutter projects and works in an orbit of the required radius. A special holder for carrying a tool in this way was marketed some years ago by Messrs. Buck & Ryan ; it consisted of a small slide-rest which could be bolted to the faceplate and enabled the eccentricity of the tool holder to be adjusted. Primarily intended for boring, it was also adaptable for face milling and similar operations within the scope of a single-point cutter.

Cutters of small diameter are sometimes made with a single cutting edge, and may often be found to work more cleanly and efficiently than ordinary milling cutters. They consist virtually of simple D-bits, ground away in certain cases to provide better front clearance or more efficient rake angle. A plain D-bit, however, works quite well as a rotary cutter for very fine precision milling at high speed, and this is the form of cutter almost universally employed in engraving machines, which may be regarded as a specialised form of vertical profile milling machine.

One very important advantage of the single-point cutter for occasional work, is the ease of making a bit, and also of sharpening it when required.

Principles of Multi-point Cutters

A cutter of this type may be regarded as the equivalent of a number of single-point tools mounted radially in a hub, all being exactly the same in form, rake and clearance angles,

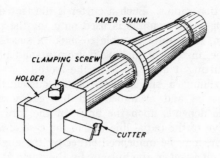

Fig. 5. Form of fly-cutter holder as used in milling machines

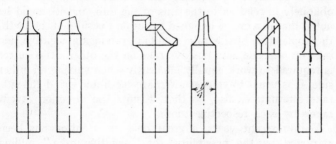

Fig. 6. Form cutters for use in cutter bar

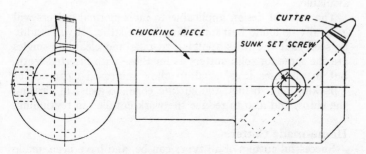

Fig. 7. Fly-cutter holder for mounting in lathe chuck

and projection radius. Such a cutter is illustrated in Fig. 8,
and although this example is used only for the purposes of
explanation, it is quite possible to make a successful cutter
of this type, instead of making it from a solid piece of tool
steel by cutting it away to form the teeth.

By examining a single tooth of the cutter, the various
angles of rake and clearance can be readily understood.
Rake angle depends upon the angle of the forward cutting
face, relative to the radial line, and in the case of an inserted-
tooth cutter, may be influenced either by the angle at which
the cutter bit is set in the hub, or by the angle at which it is
ground. Front or peripheral clearance is determined by the
angle of the outer tip of the cutter to the tangent line. Side
rake is produced by grinding the forward face of the cutter
obliquely in relation to the axis of the hub, and it should be
noted that in a cutter designed to cut on the sides of the teeth,
the application of side rake results in producing negative side
rake on one side, and positive rake on the other. If a cutter
is required to work equally efficiently when cutting on either
side, it is usual to stagger alternate teeth and grind the side
rake alternately, also, so that it suits the direction of cut
taken by each respective tooth.

Within recent years, a great deal of attention has been
attracted by the possibilities of " negative rake " milling
cutters, but it is pointed out that the real advantages of these
only apply when special machines and special tools are
available.

The rules of design applicable to more normal cutters will
generally be found best for milling in the lathe. It will readily
be seen that the rules applying to rake and clearance angles
are the same for solid cutters as for those with inserted teeth,
but in all cases it is usual to allow increased clearance or
" backing off " behind the cutting edge, to assist in clearing
the chips, and also to reduce the work entailed in regrinding.

Home-made Cutters

Successful cutters of all types can be, and have been, made
in the home workshop. For large diameter cutters, the use

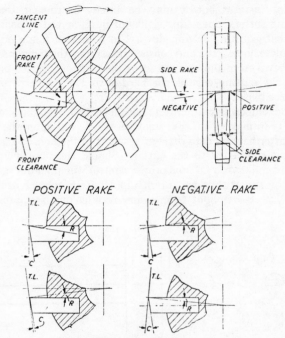

Fig. 8. Inserted-tooth milling cutter, illustrating rake and clearance angles

of inserted cutter bits of round section tool steel gives very satisfactory results, and the holders are very easily made. Cutters of the " peripheral " and " face " type, respectively, having the bits held in place by grub screws, are shown in Figs. 9 and 10. Where very little shaping or forming of the bits is required, high-speed steel bits, as used for boring bars, may be used, all ground to the same shape and size on the cutting edges, and set to project exactly equally. Silver steel, which is much more readily obtained, and also more easily shaped in the soft state before hardening, gives quite satisfactory results for occasional work, and is suitable for making cutters from the solid. The methods of hardening and tempering silver steel have been described many times in *The*

Model Engineer but it may be briefly mentioned, that for milling cutters, quenching right out in oil or water, polishing, and subsequent " letting down " in a bunsen flame or on a hot-plate, gives good and consistent results ; the temper should be drawn from the shank end in the case of inserted bits, so that the cutting edge is the hardest and other parts as soft as possible.

For tempering solid cutters with a central hole, the simplest way is to make a tapered mandrel which will enter the hole, and after heating it to redness, insert it in the hole so that the heat is conducted to the cutter. Should the temper appear to be running too fast for proper control, the mandrel may be temporarily withdrawn, or manipulated to control irregular local effects. A light to medium straw colour is suitable for

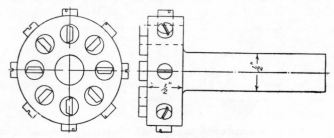

Fig. 9. Inserted-tooth face milling cutter

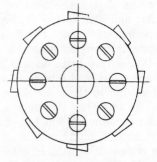

Fig. 10. Inserted-tooth peripheral
milling cutter

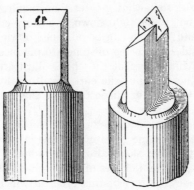

Fig. 11. Simple flat end-mill

high-speed working on soft metals, but for tough metals it may be advisable to let the cutter tips down to a dark straw.

End mills are very easily made, and the methods employed are so well known as to need little further description. The two-edged flat type of cutter is the most popular, and an example of such a cutter, with the clearance angles exaggerated for the sake of clearness, is shown in Fig. 11. This form of cutter is highly suitable for milling small keyways, and ports in cylinders. Among the points to be observed in making these cutters, it may be mentioned that the shank should be as rigid as possible, and for small diameter cutters, a standard shank of about $\frac{1}{4}$ in. minimum diameter is advisable, the actual cutting portion being no longer than is necessary for the work required, plus a reasonable margin for re-sharpening of the cutting edges. This part should not be turned down to a sharp internal corner, but a liberal fillet should be left to ensure maximum strength at this point, and to avoid the risk of hardening cracks being started. This applies also to the internal corner of the flats, which should not be formed with a flat, square-cornered file, but rounded away with a small round or half-round file, and left as smooth as possible. When filing the cutting edges, it is advisable to make the clearance angles somewhat greater than required for efficient cutting, and not to file right down to a sharp edge, but leave a narrow " land," which can be oilstoned down after hardening, the flat sides also being oilstoned to produce a keen edge. The front cutting edges of the cutter illustrated are shown square with the axis, but the cutter will usually work better if they are concave, or disposed at a slight inward angle, to relieve the centre.

Besides the plain square-cornered slotting cutter, it is possible to use the same general principle in cutters for dovetail, undercut or tee slots, also with radiused or otherwise shaped ends for certain classes of form milling. In some gear-cutting processes, cutters of this type, in which the form is produced by turning the end to a template (prior to flattening and backing off) have been used, but end milling is a rather slow process for this class of work, and the majority of gear cutting is done with peripheral cutters.

Where really high cutting efficiency is required, the simple flat end mill suffers from the disadvantage that the actual cutting edge is not truly radial, being inevitably set at a negative angle of rake, depending upon the thickness of the flat face. A very thin cutter is the most efficient, but lacks rigidity, and may be much too fragile for fast cutting. The type of cutter having two or more flutes, producing exactly radial cutting edges, is more rigid and efficient in use, and is not very difficult to make, if means are available for milling the flutes to the required shape. Three-fluted cutters can be recommended, the odd number of teeth tending to reduce chatter and produce a very clean cut.

Broken twist drills are sometimes adapted to serve as end mills, by grinding the end flat or concave, and backing off the edges ; but the results are often disappointing, due to the inherent lack of rigidity of the ordinary drill, and the fact that not only the shank, but also the upper part of the twist, are usually left soft to reduce the risk of breakage.

Chucking End Mills

All kinds of milling cutters must be securely and truly

mounted, but this applies most of all to end mills, which must necessarily overhang from the machine spindle, and cannot be supported at the outer end like side cutters mounted on an arbor. When cutters are used in the lathe, they are often held in the three-jaw chuck, which may be quite secure, but is rarely exactly true. A collet chuck is unquestionably best for holding parallel-shank cutters of all kinds, as it is the only type of chuck which holds the shank over a large surface area, and which can be maintained in true running condition under heavy duty. The small diameter over the outside of a collet chuck also facilitates accessibility and inspection of the work, without the necessity of running back the slide. Chucks of any kind should project the minimum distance from the spindle nose, so as to reduce the tendency to deflection or " spring " of the cutter under side thrust.

Backing Off Milling Cutters

In cutters of simple form, such as peripheral or side and face cutters, it is possible to machine, grind or file the teeth to shape when making the cutter from the solid, and in most· cases re-sharpening of cutters can be carried out in such a way that the essential angles are maintained constant. But in form cutters of precise and complex shape, backing off is a more difficult matter, and many ingenious methods have been devised to enable the edges to be ground or machined with proper clearance, and without affecting their correct contour. In regrinding these cutters, it is usual to grind the front cutting face only, so that neither the form nor the clearance is liable to be altered.

Inserted-tooth cutters may have the teeth ground to shape before they are inserted with the aid of a form grinding wheel, or some type of form generating or copying device, but it is the usual practice, when regrinding the teeth, to leave them *in situ* and use the same methods as for solid cutters. Some forms of cutters are designed with the teeth inset at a slight angle, so that they may be ground on a cylindrical grinder, and then reversed in their slots to produce the required clearance angles.

Slitting Saws

These are extremely useful in many kinds of light milling operations, and may be assembled in banks to make up slotting or grooving cutters of any required width. They cut more freely than solid cutters when used in this way, as the chips are broken up by the discontinuity of the cutting teeth. Small adjustments to the width of a bank of saws may be made by inserting thin metal foil or paper washers between

Fig. 12. Slitting saw

them ; the thin sliver of metal left in the cut by the separation of the saws generally breaks away and leaves only a slight roughness in the groove.

Thin slitting saws have very little lateral rigidity, and must be started very carefully in order to ensure that the cut will follow the direction intended, without being deflected sideways by spring or side pressure. The thicker cutters, however, are capable of resisting side pressure, especially if they are hollow-ground, and they are capable of taking a fine cut along one side of an already machined groove to adjust its width. Slitting saws are relatively cheap, and in view of their wide range of utility, it is worth while to keep a stock of them, in various diameters and thicknesses, always handy. (Fig. 12.)

Woodruffe-type Keyway Cutters

These are small-diameter slotting cutters formed integrally with a shank, the most popular size being ½-in. diameter on both cutter and shank, and they are made in various cutter widths. Apart from their normal use to cut keyways for " half-moon " shaft keys, they are extremely useful for many grooving and slotting jobs, and home-made cutters of this type may be varied in design to suit particular operations ; for instance, three cutters of the required width and spacing may be formed integral with a shank, to cut the steam and exhaust ports in an engine cylinder simultaneously, a much quicker process than end milling. Cutters of this type should have both sides well undercut to provide side clearance for the teeth, which cannot easily be backed off sideways.

CHAPTER III

MILLING WITHOUT SPECIAL APPLIANCES

T HE compound slide-rest of the normal type of engineers lathe provides for movements in three directions—longitudinal, crosswise and angular—all of which are in a horizontal plane. But in most milling operations some form of movement in a vertical plane is either desirable, or quite indispensable ; and to obtain such movement, some addition or attachment to the normal lathe equipment becomes necessary. With the exception of a few types of lathes in which provision is made for vertical adjustment of the slide-rest—or, in rare cases, of the headstock mandrel—milling without special attachments must necessarily be confined to operations in which vertical movements can be dispensed with.

The term "special appliance" is here taken to define an attachment or fixture devised specifically for milling purposes ; such items of equipment as angle-plates, vee blocks, machine vices, clamps and packings are considered to be included in the equipment of a normal workshop, and are not classed in the above category. With the aid of these devices, the range of milling operations which can be handled is much wider than many users of lathes may realise, and includes side and face milling, end milling, grooving and slotting, fluting, and possibly even gear cutting. In all cases the milling cutter is held in the chuck, or otherwise attached to the lathe spindle, so that the normal treadle or power drive of the lathe is utilised.

Milling Flat Surfaces

Plain flat surfaces, such as the mounting face of an engine bed-plate, or the joint face of a steam engine cylinder, can be dealt with very conveniently by a face milling process in the lathe. It may, perhaps, be observed that work of this nature is often capable of being dealt with by turning methods, or, in other words, by mounting in the lathe chuck or on the face-plate, and using a facing tool ; and if so, this is probably the most efficient method to use in such cases. But it often happens that the part being dealt with is too large or has extended projections which prevent it being swung in the lathe ; or it may happen that a projecting boss or step precludes the possibility of reaching the whole of the surface by rotating the work in this way. In such cases, the only practicable way of machining the surface is to mount the work on the cross-slide of the lathe and use a rotating cutter.

Height adjustment in work of this nature can be obtained by the use of packing, but in most cases it is not very important, the only essential point being that the diameter or sweep of the cutter should cover the width of the machined surface. In this respect, the use of a fly-cutter having adjustment for radius of the tool point, such as that shown in Fig. 7, enables the surfaces of various widths to be machined, avoiding the necessity for large diameter milling cutters, which are necessarily expensive and often difficult to keep in efficient condition.

The method of mounting work for face milling must necessarily depend to a great extent on the nature of the work, and the disposition of the bolting surfaces. If the job being handled has a flange, or other flat surface, at right angles to that which is to be milled, it is generally possible to clamp it down to the cross-slide directly, with or without the interposition of parallel packing strips to raise it to the required height to bring the centre of the milled surface approximately level with the lathe centres. Should the bolting surface be unmachined, it is necessary to ensure that it stands evenly on the cross-slide, without rocking, and squarely in relation to the vertical face ; any errors in either respect should be corrected by filing before clamping down.

An example of a component face being milled in this way is illustrated in the photograph. This is the casting for the apron of a lathe saddle, and the operation consists of milling the flat seating face for the cam-plate, which operates the clasp nut. It could not be swung in the lathe, because of the excessively large radial projection of the boss which takes the hand-wheel spindle ; and in any case, would have been awkward to mount because of the shape of the back. The top flange, designed to bolt to the underside of the lathe saddle, was, however, conveniently located to rest on a parallel packing strip on the lathe cross-slide, where it was held down by toe clamps, one of which is visible in the photograph. A side-and-face milling cutter, of sufficiently large diameter to cover the seating face on the casting, was available, but it was necessary to mount it in a rather unorthodox way, by pressing it on the shouldered end of a mandrel turned *in situ* in the lathe chuck. Normally, a cutter of this type would be clamped on the mandrel by means of a nut, but this was impracticable in the particular case, as no projection from the face could be allowed. A large diameter shell end mill, with a recessed centre to take the nut, would have been better—had it been available.

Work which is flat on both sides can usually be clamped against the vertical face of an angle-plate mounted on the cross-slide, providing that the position of the clamps can be arranged to clear the sweep of the cutter. It may, in some cases, be found necessary to drill and tap the back of the work, to take set-screws from the inside of the angle-plate, for securing the work in position. One advantage of angle-plate mounting is that it enables work to be adjusted vertically before finally clamping in position, avoiding the necessity of using packing when close adjustment of height is called for.

Small jobs can sometimes be held in the tool-post of the lathe, using the normal tool clamp to secure them in position, for facing the vertical side, or for other operations which will be described later. The use of a small machine vice, mounted either directly on the cross-slide and packed up to the

Face milling the cam seating of a lathe saddle apron

End-milling the edges of a cylinder base flange—

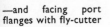
—and facing port flanges with fly-cutter

Set-up for milling recessed slide-valve face of model steam engine
cylinder

Milling bearing seatings of model steam engine

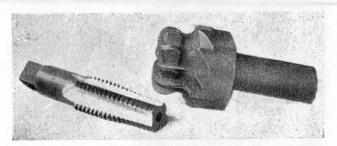

Profile cutter and finished tap

Cylinder with recessed slide-valve face, and cutter used for machining it

Milling crosshead guide bearing face of model steam engine

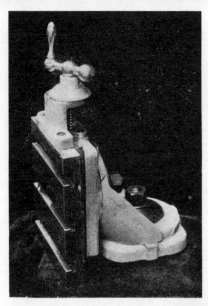

Two views of the Myford vertical slide, swivelling type

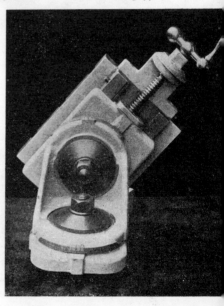

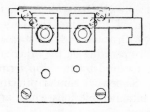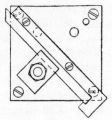

Fig. 13.   Simple jig for milling the ends of bars squarely and at an
angle respectively

required height, or on the vertical face of an angle-plate,
offers many possibilities when small parts have to be milled
on the face.

It is possible to carry out many operations which normally
call for careful and tedious fitting, by simple milling processes,
thereby improving both accuracy and speed of production.
For instance, suppose a number of bars, strips, or plates
have to be cut exactly square, or to some particular angle
at one end. It is obviously much easier to do this by milling
than by filing. The components may be clamped down to
a packing block on the cross-slide of the lathe, and set to the
correct angle by means of a square or protractor before milling
the end face. In cases where the operation is to be repeated,
a locating strip may be fitted to the packing block, or a simple
jig may be made.

Fig. 13 shows a job of this nature, in which a great saving of
time was effected in producing a number of square-section
bars, having one end square, and the other at an angle of 45
degrees. These were required in the construction of a piece
of apparatus, and all bars had to be alike, both in respect of
length and angles, so that they could be interchanged if
desired.

A flat baseplate was first made, of a suitable size to take the
bars, and capable of being mounted on the lathe cross-slide
at a convenient height for dealing with the work. On this was
mounted a locating strip, which could be secured to the plate
in either of two positions, i.e., square or 45 degrees to the edge.

The first position was used to locate the bars for facing the
ends square, toe clamps being used to secure the bars in
position ; after all had been dealt with at one end, the strip was
shifted to the angular position for operating on the other end.
Uniform length of the bars was ensured by the stop formed
at the end of the locating strip. Somewhat similar principles
may be employed to deal with innumerable jobs which arise
in the course of workshop practice.

End Milling

This differs from face milling only in that it is usually
applied only to narrow surfaces, and in the formation of
recesses and slots.   A very common application of end milling
in the lathe is in the cutting of closed keyways in shafts,
ports in cylinders of small steam and I.C. engines, and fluting
small connecting-rods, links, beams and rockers.

Height adjustment is nearly always of some importance
in end milling operations, hence it is generally desirable to
provide packing of graded thickness on which to mount the
work, or devise some means whereby work is automatically
centred or located vertically.

For cutting keyways in shafts, the latter must be held
exactly at centre height.   It is often possible to hold a shaft
in the lathe tool-post, preferably on a vee packing-block, but
it is obviously necessary to adjust the height of the packing
to suit the diameter of the shaft.   This can be avoided by
using a vee packing-block held on its side, and attaching
the work to it by clamps.   To ensure that the vee block is
exactly at the correct height, it may be milled in position by
means of a flat cutter having the end pointed at an angle of
90 degrees, before clamping the work in position.

An improved device to hold shafts for key-seating operations
is shown in Fig. 14.   It consists of an iron casting having a
slotted lug to enable it to be held down by the tool-post
stud, and a locating strip on the underside to take the thrust
of the cutter and ensure alignment with the edge of the
top-slide.   While this might, perhaps, be described as a
" special appliance," its use is not confined only to milling

operations, but may be extended to such purposes as holding boring-bars or other round section lathe tools.

An example of a milling job on which both an end mill and a single-point fly-cutter were used, is illustrated in the pair of photographs on page 25. They show a small petrol engine cylinder being milled around the edge of the base flange and on the port flange faces ; both operations are, in actual fact, face milling, but it was found convenient to employ two different types of cutters for working on the various faces.

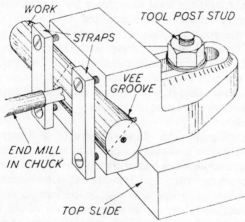

Fig. 14. Vee block clamping device for end-milling keyways in shafts

The casting was bolted directly down in an inverted position on the lathe cross-slide by a single bolt passing through the centre bore, a steel disc being used as a clamping plate. Note that paper washers are interposed between the bolting faces, a precaution which should be observed wherever possible, not only to protect the machined surfaces of the work, but also to improve the grip. As it happened, the edge of the the base flange came almost level with the lathe centres, so that no packing under the cylinder was necessary.

In milling the edges, measurements were taken from a

datum line marked off in correct relation to the port positions, and after one edge had been milled, it was used as a reference face, subsequent edges being located by squaring off this edge from the face of the lathe chuck. The exhaust and inlet port faces were at right angles to each other, and parallel with two of the edges of the flange, so that after these edges had been machined, it was only necessary to substitute the fly-cutter for the end mill to mill the flanges.

This particular job is one which could possibly have been done by turning methods, but the setting up for milling was much easier, and the total time taken for the series of operations only amounted to a few minutes.

The procedure adopted in end milling ports in small steam engine cylinders is fairly well known, having been described, with various minor differences of method, several times in the past ; but some reference to it is called for, in view of the fact that it is not only a very common operation, but involves principles applicable to a very wide variety of other work.

The drawing, Fig. 15, shows a more or less conventional cylinder block for a double-acting steam engine, as employed for locomotives, marine and stationary work, though it does not represent any particular type, nor is it necessarily drawn true to scale. The operation to be performed consists of milling the three ports in the slide-valve face of the block.

It is necessary to have available small end mills of a suitable type, and preferably of the same diameter as the width of the respective ports. Smaller diameter cutters can be used, but they involve the need for extra packings and re-setting of the work ; in addition, the ports are in most cases so narrow that it is advisable, on the grounds of mechanical strength, to use the maximum size of cutter allowable. In some cases, rotary cutters of the dental burr type are used, but while these are highly efficient, it is often difficult to run them at the proper speed in an ordinary lathe, and their small shanks leave something to be desired in the way of rigidity. Home-made flat end mills have proved highly satisfactory for this class of work ; they should have shanks not less than $\frac{1}{4}$-in.

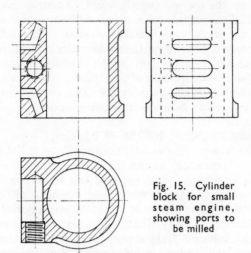

Fig. 15. Cylinder block for small steam engine, showing ports to be milled

diameter, with projecting cutting tips only just long enough for the desired depth of cut, and should be run at a speed of not less than 750 to 1,000 r.p.m. (which is as high as can be obtained on the majority of small lathes), but much higher speeds can be used to advantage. They must, of course, be securely mounted, and run dead true.

Method of Fixing

The only other fittings required are a long tee-headed bolt, to secure the cylinder block to the lathe cross-slide, with a plate or disc to span the cylinder bore, and three parallel packing blocks to raise the cylinder to the required height for the respective cuts. (Fig. 16.) Packing block A should be of such a thickness as to bring the centre line of the top port exactly coincident with the level of the lathe centres, and packing blocks B and C should be equal in thickness to the distance between the ports. The blocks may conveniently be made from discs parted off a large diameter bar of any available metal, and faced up truly on both sides. It would be an advantage to tap the centre hole in packing block A

to screw on the tee-bolt (which would, of course, have to be threaded all the way down) as this would promote firmness in locating the work, and facilitate re-setting. A further refinement would be to spigot the packing blocks to fit into each other, and also into the bore of the cylinder, as this would provide for *positive* location of the cylinder ; but the spigoted disc on the top of the cylinder does this to some extent, if the bolt is not free to move in the cross-slide.

Measuring Required Height of Packing

In order to assess the exact thickness of the initial packing block A, it is necessary to find the height of the lathe centres above the cross-slide. It is not sufficient to rely on nominal figures, and measurements made from the point of the lathe centre to the slide with a rule involve a very decided risk of error. The simplest way of obtaining a really precise measurement is as follows : Hold a piece of material in the chuck or between the centres, either turning it in position to a definite diameter, or chucking a stock size bar or mandrel to run dead truly. Measure the distance between the bar and the cross-slide by means of a pair of inside calipers, or by the use of slip gauges and feelers. The height of the centre above the cross-slide will, of course, be equal to this measurement, plus the radius of the turned bar ; for example, if the bar used is ¾-in. diameter, and the distance between it and the slide is 1 9/16 in., the centre height will be 1 15/16 in. If, in the present instance, the first port to be milled is ⅞ in. from the *lower* face of the cylinder block, the height of packing block A will have to be 1 1/16 in. to raise the block to the height required for milling the port.

Setting up

The slide-valve face of the cylinder is first set dead square with the lathe axis, which may be done either by measurement from the lathe chuck or faceplate, or by using a square set against a parallel mandrel temporarily placed between centres. Having secured the cylinder, the cutter is placed in the chuck, and the milling operation carried out by means

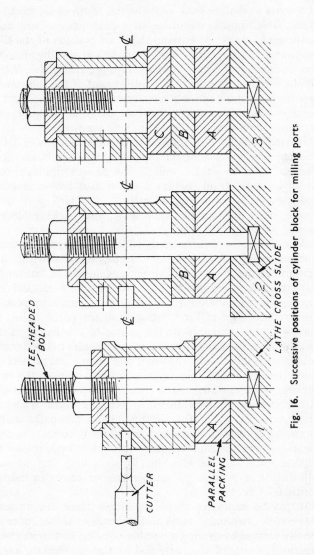

Fig. 16. Successive positions of cylinder block for milling ports

of a series of shallow cuts, each the full width of the port. It is advisable to make use of the cross-slide index, or any other convenient means of verifying the exact position of the slide, to ensure that the cutter neither runs short nor digs into the end on successive cuts ; positive stops are still better, if they can be fitted to the slide. The adjustment of the slide should be rather tighter than is normally used for turning, and all possible precautions taken to avoid shake or backlash, and promote rigidity, in any kind of milling operation in the lathe.

Having completed one port, the cylinder block is removed, packing block *B* placed on top of *A*, and the work again replaced and re-set for milling the second (middle) port, which in most steam engines is wider than the outer ports, and thus calls for a larger cutter. The third port is, of course, dealt with in the same way, with packing block *C* used in addition to *A* and *B*.

A variation in this method, which is preferred by some workers, enables packing block *C* to be dispensed with. The first and second ports are dealt with as described, but for the third port, packing block *B* is removed, and the cylinder block turned upside down. This method, however, is liable to introduce error in the positioning of the ports, unless the middle port is precisely in the centre of the length of the block. Any discrepancy in this respect results in the distance between the middle and the outer ports being unsymmetrical, to the extent of *twice* the error. The provision of the extra packing block, to allow of working from one reference face of the cylinder block only, is, therefore, worth while. A slight error in the initial setting does not usually matter much if the *relative* position of the ports is correct, because the usual small steam engine is provided with means for adjusting the slide-valve bodily up or down ; but no such adjustment is possible to compensate for errors in relative positions of ports.

It may be mentioned that the passages which communicate between the two outer ports and the ends of the cylinder are usually formed by drilling a number of holes, in a row extending the breadth of the port, and at the appropriate angle ;

but it would be quite practicable to form them by end milling, if a fixture were made to hold the cylinder block at the correct angle and height for this operation. A milled passage would provide the maximum area of steam way, and avoid abrupt changes of shape and area, thus promoting efficiency in the flow of steam at high velocity.

The methods described are equally practicable for milling ports in cylinders of small two-stroke I.C. engines, or for many other purposes where slots, grooves or steps at specified distances are called for.

In end milling slots or grooves which cannot be finished at one height setting, operators find it difficult to attain exactly the same depth of cut on successive lateral cuts. Whenever possible, some positive means of locating the work on the saddle, such as backing it up with an angle-plate or vee block clamped to the cross-slide, should be adopted ; and by ensuring that the work is always in the same place relative to the saddle, depth may be gauged by means of the lead screw index, or by a positive stop clamped to the lathe bed. But when this method is impracticable, here is a simple method by means of which exact depth gauging can be ensured.

Before starting the first cut, run the work up close to the cutter, so that a piece of thin paper (such as a cigarette paper) interposed between the two is just barely held in position. Note the position of the lead screw index, and then proceed with the cut to the required depth, noting the index reading when the required depth is attained. On successive cuts, the same procedure is adopted, and if the same difference in the index figures is applied each time, the cuts will all be exactly equal in depth.

Fluting Connecting Rods

Beams, links, levers and rods are often grooved or fluted to enable the maximum strength in relation to weight to be obtained. Work of this nature can usually be carried out by end milling, if means are available for holding the component in the required position on the cross-slide.

This can often be done by clamping to the vertical side of an angle-plate, as described for face milling operations. In cases where the groove or flute is tapered, a cut can first be taken along one side, after which the work is readjusted at the correct angle and height to suit the other edge, and a cut taken to exactly the same depth.

A very simple fixture for milling rods or links which have drilled eyes at the two ends, with a fluted portion between them, can be made by clamping a flat or square bar in the lathe tool-post, so that the face is exactly vertical, and drilling bolt or stud holes at the centre distance of the eyes, and exactly level with the lathe centres. This can be done in position, using a centre-drill in the lathe chuck to start the holes truly, and following up with a larger drill as required. When the component is held in place, using bolts or studs which fit the eyes closely, it will be located correctly for milling the flute exactly in alignment with the eye centres.

The form of connecting-rod shown in Fig. 17 is one which is very commonly found in small I.C. engine practice, and as castings or forgings in suitable materials for this purpose are not normally available, it is usually necessary to machine them from the solid. A simple method of setting up these rods on two studs, as above described, but with provision for milling the tapered flute, is illustrated in Fig. 18. The essential point about this method is that while the stud at the little end of the rod is made to fit the eye closely, that at the big end is made smaller than the eye, so that the rod can be swung up or down to the required angle to form the tapered flutes. The first cut produces a groove parallel to one edge of the rod, and the second runs parallel to the other edge; both cuts must be taken to exactly the same depth. If the taper is very pronounced, a noticeable projection is left in the centre of the flute, adjacent to the big end boss ; but this can be removed by slackening the studs just sufficiently to enable the rod to be worked up and down, while running the cutter in the end of the flute.

In a variation of this method, a cutter of small diameter can be used to mill the sides of the flute, which can be formed

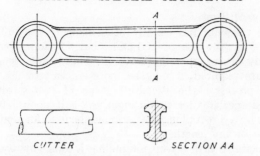

CUTTER   SECTION AA

Fig. 17. Connecting-rod for I.C. engine, showing typical section, and form of fluting cutter employed

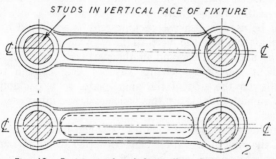

STUDS IN VERTICAL FACE OF FIXTURE

Fig. 18. Positions of rod for milling flute in two operations

in such a way as to extend around the sides of the bosses, removing considerably more superfluous metal than is possible with the round-ended flute. The centre of the flute is then milled out with a cutter of larger diameter.

The form of cutter used for this work should be as shown in Fig. 17, the sides being tapered to an included angle of about 10 degrees, and the end slightly rounded. On no account should a sharp-cornered cutter be used for fluting connecting-rods, or it will defeat the purpose of obtaining maximum strength for minimum weight. The characteristic " dumb bell "-shaped cross-section of a rod fluted on both sides, by the methods described, is also shown in this figure.

Keyway Milling

Some reference has already been made to the milling of keyways by the use of end mills, but for some purposes, especially where open keyways of considerable length or depth are required, it may be more efficient to use a side milling process. The Woodruffe type of cutter, although intended specially for producing the " half-moon " form of keyway by a direct plunge cut, can also be used for continuous keyways of any length.

An example of a set-up for milling a long keyway, using either a Woodruffe cutter or any other form of slotting cutter of appropriate width, is illustrated in Fig. 19. It will be seen that the main mounting fixture is a standard angle-plate, though any other vertical block or bracket might be used, and a vee packing strip is employed to locate the shaft against the vertical face. One or more bolts or clamps may be used, and in the particular case illustrated, the bent end of the clamp was not long enough to bear directly on the side of the angle-plate, so a packing strip, thick enough to make up this deficiency, was interposed under the heel.

Further examples of operations which can be carried out with the aid of an angle-plate or other vertical mounting fixture are shown on pages 26 and 27. Both operations are encountered in the machining of components for a well-known type of model horizontal steam engine. In the first case, the flat surface of the main casting, which forms the lower bearing surface for the crosshead slide, is being face-milled. The casting, having been filed or machined flat on the under surface, is clamped against the vertical face of the angle-plate by means of a pair of small G-clamps, the height being adjusted to bring the centre of the surface to be milled approximately level with the lathe centres, though this adjustment is not critical, so long as the cutter is slightly larger in diameter than the width of the milled surface.

This particular operation could have been dealt with by mounting on the lathe faceplate and using a facing tool, but as the surface is not symmetrical with the length of the casting, it would have called for a greater radius of swing and a wider gap than is usually provided in small lathes. The alternative methods of dealing with it would have been by shaping or filing, neither of which is quite so easy or convenient as milling for the average model engineer.

In the next photograph, the same casting is being dealt with, but in this case the operation consists of milling the slots for the main-bearing seatings. The angle-plate is in this case up-ended so that it rests on its side edges (care should be taken to see that these are square with the faces both ways) and is held down on the cross-slide by two toe clamps, which engage the slots of the angle-plate as shown. The casting is held to the angle-plate by a single bolt passing through a cored hole between the bearing standards, a strap being used to straddle the raised side edges. In this operation,

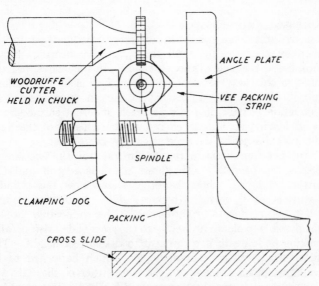

Fig. 19. Milling keyway in shaft by clamping the latter against the side of a vertical fixture

height adjustment is more critical, but is easily set by tapping the casting into position before tightening the bolt. It is also possible to move the casting slightly, to adjust the width of the slots, in this way, should the end mill used be too narrow to form them in one cut ; but it is better to avoid the necessity for this if possible, as it introduces a potential source of error.

If there is much metal to be machined out to form the slots, it is advisable to start with a smaller cutter, say 1/16 in. less in diameter than the finished size, and use the correct size cutter to finish the sides. A large facing cutter should be used to face the tops of the bearing horns to provide a flat surface for the keep plates or bearing caps. When setting up work of this nature, a centre line should be marked across the full width of the casting, and carefully checked up against a true-running point centre in the lathe for height and squareness.

Recessed Valve-chests

Some steam engines have an integral valve-chest in the main cylinder casting, with the slide-valve bearing surface sunk below the level of the joint face. In such cases, practically the only way to machine this surface is by end milling, and it is frequently necessary to use an angular-sided or " dovetail " cutter, in order to reach undercut surfaces, and avoid leaving an untouched radius at each end of the limit of travel allowed by the aperture in the valve-chest.

An operation of this nature is illustrated in the two photographs, on page 26. One shows the finished job and the cutter employed, while the other shows how the cylinder casting is set up on the lathe cross-slide. As the casting had a flat bolting face at right-angles to the slide-valve face, it was possible to clamp it directly to the cross-slide, with parallel packing underneath it to bring it to the correct height. The cutter used was a ready-made one which happened to be available, but a home-made end mill, either of the flat two-blade type or a more elaborate multi-toothed cutter mounted on a shank, would have served equally well.

It may be observed that most model steam engines are made with a detached " picture frame " type of steam-chest, which makes it possible to machine the slide-valve surface much more easily; but similar machining problems to those involved in the above operation frequently crop up in model engineering practice, even if they do not occur in cylinder machining.

Side Milling Cylinder Ports

Before dismissing the subject of machining small steam engine cylinders, reference may be made to a method of milling the ports in the slide-valve bearing face, which is less common than the end milling method already described, but has advantages in certain circumstances. It consists in the use of a side milling cutter, similar to a small slotting or Woodruffe key-cutter, which produces a crescent-shaped slot of limited depth in relation to its width, but generally deep enough for all practical purposes.

The cylinder is mounted on the lathe cross-slide, the bore axis being horizontal and the slide-valve face vertical, with the centre line of ports on the same level as the lathe centres. A convenient method of mounting is to clamp the block to the vertical side of an angle-plate by a single bolt passing through the bore. It is essential to use a cutter having a small shank diameter, to obtain the maximum depth of cut in relation to port width, and for this reason arbor-mounted cutters are generally unsuitable. Cutters formed integral with the shank are best, but it is practicable to extend the shank beyond the cutter, so that it can be supported by the tailstock centre. A standard Woodruffe key-seating cutter cannot be used unless the shoulder of the shank is turned away behind the cutter to provide extra clearance.

It will readily be seen that three ports (or more if necessary) can be cut simultaneously by this method, by " ganging " the three cutters, of appropriate width, and spaced at the correct distance apart, as shown in Fig. 20. Besides being quicker than end milling, this method produces certain accuracy in the width and spacing of the ports, and has practical advantages for repetition work. The square-cut ends of the ports may be preferred to the rounded ends of ports produced by end milling.

Screw-heading

Many operations such as the slotting, flatting, or squaring of screw heads can be carried out with the minimum of special equipment. The work can often be held in the lathe toolpost, with the aid of a vee packing strip, so that its centre is level with that of the lathe centres, but in many cases the provision of a simple chucking device will be found helpful. A cheap drill chuck, with a parallel shank, clamped in a split holder similar to that used for boring bars, will enable small-diameter screws to be held quite firmly enough for slotting the heads, and without damaging the threads where held directly by the chuck jaws, though obviously, a more elaborate screw chuck would be better. (See Fig. 21.)

For squaring heads of tool screws, or the shanks of taps, reamers, valves, etc., some simple method of indexing the work in four positions is obviously desirable. A very elementary device, which serves its purpose quite effectively, is to mount a square plate temporarily on the shank by any convenient means, such as by driving or soft-soldering it on. It need not necessarily be concentrically true with the shaft. By means of a square or spirit level, the four flats on the plate are successively located for milling the flats on the work, and the depth of cut is measured by means of the lathe top-slide index. Similar methods can, of course, be used for forming a hexagonal head on a valve cap or screw plug, by using a guide plate of appropriate shape, and in cases where the production of more elaborate indexing devices is not considered worth while, will be found reasonably accurate—at least, much more so than filing, unless the worker is very highly skilled in the latter art.

It is possible to halve the number of operations needed for producing a square or hexagon, by using two cutters spaced a distance apart equal to the diameter across flats of the finished form. This is a very practical means of speeding up the

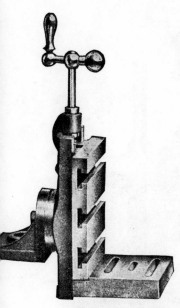

Senior vertical slide with horizontal angle bracket

Two types of cutter frames made and used by Mr. K. N. Harris

Slotting holes in cam-plate seating of lathe apron

Milling keyway in spindle of the " M.E." drilling machine

Slot milling the jockey pulley lug on headstock casting of the
" M.E." drilling machine

A light milling spindle with slide and sensitive feed, by Mr. K. N. Harris

Mr. Harris's milling spindle in use on a 4-in. Spencer lathe

The Potts milling and drilling spindle

The milling and drilling spindle, as shown in Fig. 38, in use on a Myford ML4 lathe

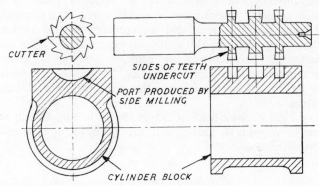

CUTTER

SIDES OF TEETH UNDERCUT

PORT PRODUCED BY SIDE MILLING

CYLINDER BLOCK

Fig. 20. Method of cutting ports in steam engine by side milling

operation, which is worth while in repetition work, but saves hardly any time in a " one-off " job, because it is necessary to set the work very carefully to ensure a symmetrical cut. If, however, the method is adopted, the best way to centralise the work is to turn a small projection on the end of it, to the diameter across flats, and adjust the work for milling so that this part just passes between the cutters. After milling, the projection is, of course, machined away.

The type of cutter most suitable for milling flats, squares and hexagons on work of this nature is a " side and face " cutter of the appropriate hand. Where two cutters are used

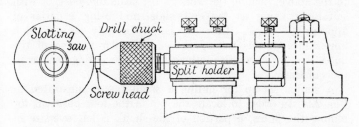

Slotting saw

Drill chuck

Split holder

Screw head

Fig. 21. Screw held in drill chuck, mounted in toolpost by means of a split holder, for slotting operation on head

simultaneously, they should be of opposite hand. For occasional jobs, working on one side only, large diameter end mills may be used, and an ordinary slotting cutter, without side teeth, is also quite serviceable if the sides are relieved by undercutting or concave grinding. As the direction of cutting thrust is mostly downwards, the work may be fed in from the front, with normal direction of lathe rotation.

The form of work-holding fixture shown in Fig. 14 will be found very useful for dealing with many jobs of the type now under discussion.

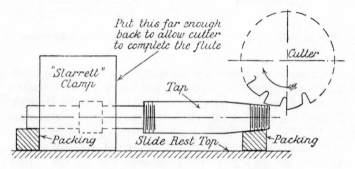

Fig. 22.   Tap held on slide-rest of lathe for milling flutes

Fluting Taps and Reamers

These operations can also be carried out in similar manner to the above, holding the work in the lathe tool-post, or with suitable packing on the cross-slide, and using a cutter of appropriate shape. Indexing is not usually of very high importance in this work ; indeed, irregular spacing of the flutes is often a practical advantage in preventing chatter in tools of this class.

A simple set-up for fluting a small tap is illustrated in Fig. 22. In order to locate the tap in the four positions for milling the flutes, a portion of the shank is left oversize in diameter, and this is filed square, the flats being taken down flush with the rest of the shank. (This is, of course, machined

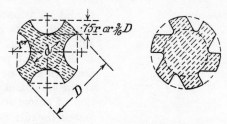

Fig. 23. Cross-section of standard four-fluted tap, and six-fluted master tap or hob, respectively

away after cutting the flutes, and before hardening and tempering the tap.)

A small machine vice or toolmaker's clamp can be used to hold the tap, the entire assembly being mounted on a flat baseplate on the top or cross-slide of the lathe, with the ends of the tap mounted on suitable packing blocks to raise it to the correct height for fluting. Soft metal or fibre packing blocks will be found best, and they may with advantage be vee-notched to assist in location and prevent them being shaken out under vibration. Before finally tightening the vice, bed the work well down on the packings by tapping with a hide or lead mallet.

It is always desirable to feed the work against the rotation of the cutter, so that in dealing with a job of this nature, it

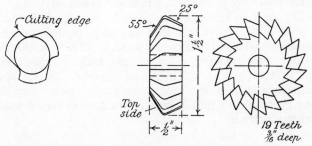

Fig. 24. Cross-section of three-fluted tap, and cutter used for fluting same

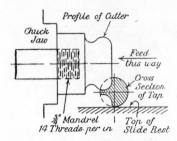

Fig. 25. Showing how a profile cutter can be used for tap fluting

should be mounted at the back end of the cross-slide and fed towards the front. If this is not practicable, the work may be mounted at the front and the direction of cutter rotation reversed, the cutter also being turned round on its shank so that the teeth face the right way ; but if this is done, it is best to mount the cutter in a collet chuck, or fix it in some way so that it cannot loosen under the effect of left-hand rotation.

The cross-section of the ordinary four-fluted tap is shown in Fig. 23, and this can be cut with a standard radius-forming tool. A three-fluted tap is often fluted to the shape shown in Fig. 24, which calls for a rather different form of cutter, as shown in the same illustration. It is, however, possible to flute taps with cutters of other shapes ; in some cases it may be found possible to obtain a better shape of flute by offsetting the cutter from the centre line of the work.

Fig. 25 shows how an odd profile cutter was utilised to machine a four-fluted tap, and the photograph on page 27 shows that the result was satisfactory. Reamers or milling cutters may be fluted with a plain " side and face " cutter offset to produce a " ratchet " form of tooth. In dealing with all kinds of cutting tools, care should be taken to position the cutter in such a way as to produce rake and clearance angles of the correct " hand." It is very awkward to find, after spending a lot of time making a right-hand tap, that it cuts in a left-handed direction, or *vice versa*. Reamers will, of course, work equally well either way, but most operators will find it awkward to have to turn a reamer backwards in use.

CHAPTER IV

THE VERTICAL SLIDE

ALTHOUGH the principles of holding and setting-up work described in the previous section can be applied to many other operations than those illustrated, the facility and convenience of a working adjustment in a vertical or oblique plane will nearly always be apparent ; and in many cases it becomes almost or entirely a necessity. For instance, it is commonly necessary to carry out a side milling operation in which there is no clear path of approach to the cut, and the relative vertical position of work and cutter must be altered to clear an obstacle. This condition arises when side milling the flutes of a locomotive connecting-rod, where only the portion of the rod between the eyes must be fluted, and the cut must run out on the radius of the cutter, adjacent to the bosses at each end. Clearly, an operation of this nature cannot be carried out without some form of vertical adjustment ; in this case, the amount of movement required is quite small, but in other operations, it may be fairly considerable, up to a matter of one or two inches ; beyond this amount, it is doubtful whether the small lathe, of the type commonly used for model engineering, is adequate to deal with the work.

Before describing the orthodox types of vertical slide, it may be noted that some lathes intended for the use of model engineers have incorporated means of adjusting the effective elevation of the cross-slide to provide a certain range of vertical adjustment. The best known example of this device is found in the 4-in. round-bed Drummond lathe, where the effect of swinging the saddle around the bed is utilised for this purpose. It will readily be seen, from the illustration shown in Fig. 26, that this is equivalent to swinging the head-stock mandrel of the lathe in an arc about the bed centre ; the highest position of the mandrel being obtained when the cross-slide is at right angles to the connecting centre line between mandrel and bed centres. Any other position reduces the distance between the cross-slide and the mandrel, constitut-ing, in effect, a means of vertical adjustment.

Another very simple but ingenious cross-slide adjustment was provided as an accessory to the Jackson-Rigby lathe, in which a special form of cross-slide, complete with its slideway (or soleplate) and lead screw, was hinged to the saddle at the back, and provided with an elevating screw at the front, so that it could be tilted up to effect vertical adjustment (Fig. 27). It has often been suggested that a tilting cross-slide table is impracticable, on the grounds that it will pro-duce a taper cut ; but this is only true when the tilt is applied to a separate and superimposed fixture, such as a sine table.

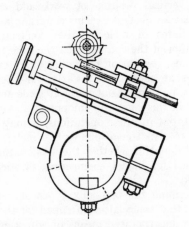

Fig. 26. Method of adjusting effective height of cross slide on 4-in. round-bed Drummond lathe

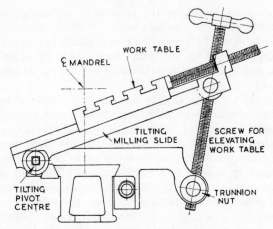

Fig. 27. Tilting cross-slide provided for milling on Jackson-Rigby lathe

So long as the plane of motion of the cross-slide is kept parallel to the bolting surface, the cut will also run parallel to this surface, whatever the angle of tilt. Incidentally, this principle is applied to milling machine practice in the Kendall and Gent tilting-bed horizontal miller.

To avoid possible embarrassment to either manufacturers or readers, it should be explained that neither the Jackson-Rigby lathes nor the Drummond 4-in. round bed lathes are now in production, though a limited stock of spares for the latter is held by the Myford Engineering Co. Ltd., Beeston, Notts.

It is rather beside the point to enumerate the many elaborate devices which have been incorporated in lathe design at various times, such as elevating headstocks or vertical saddle slides, since very few readers will have access to lathes incorporating them.

The Vertical Slide

Apart from devices actually incorporated in the design of the lathe, the handiest attachment which can be fitted to an ordinary lathe, for the purpose of providing vertical adjustment, is the well-known "vertical slide." This device is produced by various makers of lathes and accessories, in a range of sizes to suit lathes from about $2\frac{1}{2}$-in. to 6-in. centres, and in more or less elaborate and adaptable forms of design.

Basically, the vertical slide consists of a simple slide-rest, comparable to the normal lathe cross-slide, and usually provided with tee slots or other means of holding work, which is attached to a right-angled bracket adapted to be mounted on the lathe cross-slide, so that the plane of movement of the subsidiary slide is in a vertical plane. The base of the angle bracket is usually capable of being swivelled around a vertical centre pivot, and in some cases, the subsidiary slide can also be swivelled around a horizontal pivot. Slides thus equipped are capable of universal or "spherical" angular adjustment in any plane.

"Robbing Peter to Pay Paul"

It may be mentioned that in some lathes, the advantage of the vertical slide has been obtained without the addition of a subsidiary slide, by the provision of a suitable bracket, mountable on the cross-slide, and carrying the swivelling top-slide in a vertical or angular plane. While this fitting may be found extremely useful in some cases, especially if the top-slide is of ample size and equipped with tee slots, it may possibly restrict the scope of operations by depriving the lathe of one of its normal adjustments, or "robbing Peter to pay Paul." The position is somewhat different when an *extra* slide happens to be available for fitting up in this way ; but generally speaking, a vertical slide specifically designed for its purpose is the more convenient and efficient.

Apart from the early use of these devices for ornamental turning, the makers of horological and instrument lathes were the first to realise the possibilities of the vertical slide, and nearly all well-known makers of precision lathes, for this class of work, listed vertical slides among their range of equipment. Among the pioneers in the production of vertical slides in this country was the late Mr. George Adams, and his beautifully-made products are often seen at work nowadays in the more elaborately-equipped model workshops.

Somewhat more rugged, but none the less accurate, vertical slides have been manufactured for many years by Tom Senior, of Atlas Works, Liversedge, Yorks. The simplest form of fitting is illustrated in Fig. 28, and it will be seen that the upright member of the angle bracket forms the slideway for the vertical slide, so that the movement of the latter is restricted to a vertical plane in both sideways and crosswise directions. As mentioned above, however, the need is often felt for a swivelling movement of the vertical slide about a horizontal centre, and this is provided by the swivelling type of fitting illustrated in Fig. 29. At the moment, the Senior slides are temporarily out of production, but it is hoped that they will again be available to model engineers in due course. A Senior vertical slide is illustrated on page 45.

The latest Myford vertical slides are made in both swivelling and non-swivelling types, and are supplied with bases and swivels graduated in degrees, and screws indexed in thousandths of an inch travel. Two views of the swivelling type will be found on page 28. Other refinements in this make of vertical slide include a renewable nut for the lead screw, and large diameter friction pads for the pivot bolts, to prevent slipping of the swivel bases in use. These slides are designed primarily for use on the Myford 3$\frac{1}{8}$-in. and 3$\frac{1}{2}$-in. lathes, but can be applied equally well to most other lathes having a flat surface on the cross-slide to enable them to be mounted thereon.

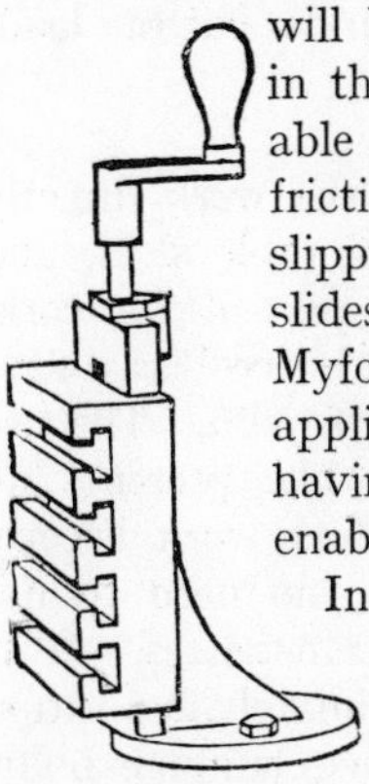

In some types of lathes, particularly those not equipped with a flat cross-slide or boring table, it is difficult or impracticable to fit the normal type of vertical slide,

Fig. 28. Early type of Senior vertical slide without swivelling adjustment

but in most cases the makers of the lathes can supply a specially-designed vertical slide, or it may be possible to adapt a standard slide, by modifying the base, or equipping it with a special sub-base.

When obtaining a vertical slide for use on any type of lathe, the user should take care to select the size and form best suited to his particular purpose. It is generally found advisable to use a heavily-built slide, with a table surface large enough to facilitate holding the largest job one is likely to deal with ; but this should not be overdone, as it is futile to fit a vertical slide out of proportion to the size and structure of the lathe to which it is attached. The choice between a swivelling and non-swivelling type of slide is often a very difficult one, because, while the extra adaptability of the former is beyond question, and may be the deciding factor in the ability to tackle a particular job, its rigidity is almost inevitably somewhat inferior to that of the non-swivelling type, and this again may be the deciding factor in the capacity limitation of the appliance. It has already been mentioned that elaboration of milling appliances can only be obtained at the expense of rigidity, and obviously, the more slides, pivots, swivels or other articulated parts contained in a milling appliance, the greater liability of the work to spring, or shift permanently from its set position, under cutting load.

Attaching Work to Vertical Slide

Whenever possible, it is best to clamp the work directly to the vertical slide, using tee-bolts in the table slots, and straps or toe clamps over some convenient part of the work. Simplicity and security of work-holding devices is always desirable, to reduce overhang and liability to slip. The use of vee blocks, parallel packings, and the like presents no essential differences to that applied in attaching work directly to the cross-slide, but there is, of course, no need to use " adjusting packings " under normal circumstances. It is usually desirable to set work at least approximately in position on the slide table, and partially tighten the clamping bolts, before setting up the vertical slide on the lathe, because otherwise, the manipulation of work, clamps, bolts and packings on a vertical surface, with everything all loose, may call for the manual equipment of a spider or an octopus.

A small machine vice which can be attached to the vertical slide is often very useful for holding small parts, especially those which have no convenient bolting surfaces. Sometimes vertical slides incorporating a vice in the structure of the table are encountered, and if this can be done without detracting from the rigidity of the slide as a whole, it is obviously a desirable feature. An angle-plate built into or securely attached to the slide table is also very useful for dealing with parts having only a horizontal bolting surface.

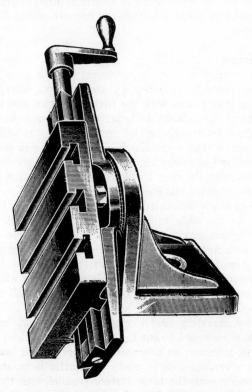

Fig. 29.   Senior vertical slide, with horizontal swivel

In addition to the use of the vertical slide as a work-holding fixture, it is equally applicable to carrying milling and drilling spindles, dividing attachments, and similar appliances, when these are not equipped with their own means of vertical adjustment, and it is necessary to provide such means to deal with particular operations.

It will be fairly evident that most of the operations described in the previous section can be performed with greater facility and convenience by using the vertical slide, as this eliminates the need for packing as a means of height adjustment, and provides a means of traversing in a vertical direction, either to adjust the width of cut or to take two or more cuts at different height levels.

Port Cutting

This advantage is particularly useful in such cases as the milling of ports in cylinders by the method described in Fig. 16, as it dispenses with the packing blocks, and enables the height of the cylinder to be adjusted for each successive port position by traversing the vertical slide. It will, however, be noted that a certain degree of rigidity is sacrificed by this method of mounting, and there may be greater difficulty in securing the cylinder block to the slide in the correct position for carrying out the milling operation.

In the example illustrated in Fig. 30, the cylinder block is attached to the slide table by means of two small angle-brackets (which may be cut from a length of angle section material of appropriate size) and a single bolt through the cylinder bore. This holds the work more rigidly than is usually possible with a single angle-plate of the size which can comfortably be accommodated on the table of a small vertical slide. Location and spacing of the ports are, of course, effected by elevating or lowering the slide table, and the cross-slide is traversed to cut the ports to the required width.

There is, however, an alternative way of dealing with this job when a vertical slide is used. The latter is mounted on the cross-slide with the table surface parallel with the lathe centres as shown in Fig. 31, and a single bolt, passing through

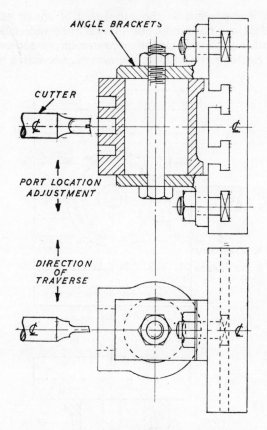

ANGLE BRACKETS

CUTTER

PORT LOCATION
ADJUSTMENT

DIRECTION
OF
TRAVERSE

Fig. 30. Steam cylinder-block mounted on vertical
slide for milling ports

the cylinder bore as before, is used to secure it to the slide,
with the port face in a vertical plane. In this way, the cross-
slide is used to adjust the location and spacing of the ports,
and the vertical slide used to traverse the work across the
cutter to produce the required width of the ports.

Whichever method is used, accuracy in port location and

spacing now depends on the adjustment of one or other of the slides, and the careful use of either the slide index, or some other positive means of measurement, is necessary to ensure correct setting. It is also necessary to watch out for

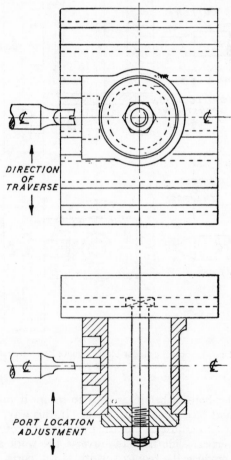

Fig. 31. An alternative way of mounting cylinder for port milling

any possibility of the adjustments shifting under vibration ; tightening up the gibs of all working slides, so that they work stiffly, is a wise precaution, and it may sometimes be found desirable to lock them positively in a set position.

End Fluting and Slotting

In fluting connecting-rods by end milling methods, the tapering of the flutes can be arranged very easily if a vertical slide having provision for swivelling about a horizontal pivot is employed. The swivel is first adjusted so that the top side of the flute is horizontal, and after cutting this side the required depth, readjustment of the swivel to bring the lower side horizontal, and a second cut to the same depth, completes the operations.

Sometimes it is much easier to set up work on the vertical slide than to set up a stationary bolting fixture. This was so in the case illustrated in the photograph on page 46, which was a further operation on the lathe apron, and consisted in milling the slots for the lifting pins of the half-nuts, which pass completely through the seating of the cam-plate. The illustration is largely self-explanatory, but it may be mentioned that in this and other photographs taken for explanatory purposes, the cutter projects farther from the chuck than is desirable from the practical point of view ; the object being to enable the essential parts to be seen more easily. As already explained, cutters should always be held as close up to the cutting edge as possible, to facilitate rigidity.

Another slot-milling operation which was conveniently dealt with by mounting the work on the vertical slide is shown on page 48, namely, the slotting of the jockey pulley lug on the headstock of the " Model Engineer " drilling machine. This operation necessitated holding the casting at an angle of 45 degrees to the plane of the column and spindle centre lines, so as to bring the centre of the slot horizontal. Several methods of securing the work to the vertical slide were practicable, the most convenient in the particular circumstances being by the use of small angle-brackets and a bolt through the bore of the casting, as shown.

Before setting up the work, the centre line for the slot was marked out, and a previously marked centre line, through the spindle and column centres, was used for setting the casting truly parallel to the surface of the vertical slide table. To bring the centre line of the slot horizontal, the swivelling adjustment of the slide was used, this adjustment being checked by means of a scribing block laid on the lathe bed, with the scriber point set exactly to centre height.

In order to reduce the amount of work entailed in milling the slot, a drill was first used to produce a row of holes closely spaced across the width of the slot and almost its full diameter. The end mill was then employed to produce a continuous slot, a larger-sized end mill being used to face the surface of the lug, and a " rose-bit " or countersink used to produce the seatings for locating the jockey pulley spindle. Both the latter operations were repeated on the other side of the casting.

When cutting keyways in shafts, either by end or side milling, the vertical slide not only provides location or depth of cut adjustment, but also a very convenient mounting to locate the shaft so that it is easily secured by a single light clamp. This is done by making use of one of the tee slots in the table in lieu of a vee block, as shown in the photograph, on page 47, which illustrates the cutting of the keyway in the spindle of the " M.E." drilling machine. As the edges of the tee slots are slightly chamfered, and it is not necessary to use very great pressure on the clamp, bruising of the shaft is avoided, but if highly-finished work is being dealt with, a slip of copper or aluminium foil may be interposed to protect the surface. In the example shown, a slip of sheet fibre was placed between the work and the toe of the clamp, but no packing was used in the tee slot. The cutter, incidentally, is a home made one, machined from silver steel in one piece, including the shank ; it has six teeth, filed by hand, and it has been used for many and diverse operations, including cutting ports in steam engine cylinders.

In cutting keyways by this method, it is important that the cutter should be properly centred, otherwise the keyway will be " out of square," or more correctly, radially offset

Potts milling attachment with cylindrical vertical slide

Adaptation of the Potts spindle to fit 3½-in. Drummond " M " type lathe

Arrangement of cutter spindle for generating cam profiles, as used by
Mr. D. H. Chaddock

Spindle with bevel reduction gear and steady bearing for use in cutting
spur gears

Arrangement of spindle and vertical slide, with work mounted on cross slide

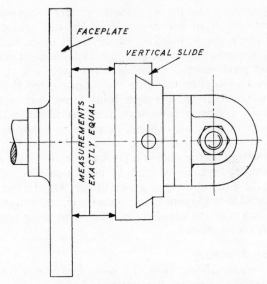

FACEPLATE

VERTICAL SLIDE

MEASUREMENTS EXACTLY EQUAL

Fig. 32. Setting vertical slide at right-angles to lathe axis

relative to the shaft. When possible, it is a good idea to present the cutter to the end face of the shaft, where its crosswise position can be measured from both sides; the provision of a temporary " pip " at the end of the shaft, equal in diameter to the width of the cutter, is a great help in setting. If, however, it is not practicable to use this method, due to insufficient traversing scope, or other means, measurement may be taken from one side of the shaft to the cutter, using a depth gauge set to half the diameter of the shaft, less half the width of the cutter. Care must, however, be taken to keep the gauge quite square with the work, to avoid the possibility of a false reading.

The squareness of the table surface of the slide, relative to the lathe axis, is also highly important in this and many other operations. A very sound method of setting up the slide to ensure this is illustrated in Fig. 32, in which it will be seen that the faceplate of the lathe is used as a reference surface (assuming that it runs quite truly), and measurements taken from the front and rear sides of the slide surface, as close to the edges as possible, by means of inside callipers or other accurate means of gauging. Measurement with a rule is not good enough. Sometimes it is possible to run the slide up into actual contact with the faceplate, but if this is done, the possibility of the slide being forced out of truth when finally tightened down should not be overlooked, and a check-up with callipers should be made to guard against this.

When setting up the slide in a position parallel to the lathe axis, a similar check can be made by using a parallel mandrel between the lathe centres, as shown in Fig. 33. In this case it is assumed that the centres are properly aligned for parallel turning, and that the mandrel, in addition to being parallel, runs truly on its centres.

Checking Accuracy

Most vertical slides, even the most inexpensive makes, are reasonably accurate, but nothing should be taken for granted in this respect when setting up the slide for an

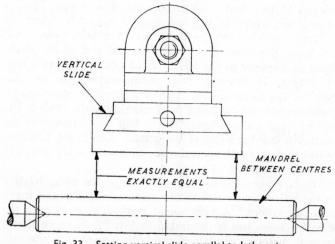

Fig. 33. Setting vertical slide parallel to lathe axis

operation which calls for a close limit of precision. A slight burr or a speck of swarf under the foot of the slide may throw it out of truth on the vertical face ; or the surface of the cross-slide may not be perfectly parallel with the lathe axis. The perpendicular accuracy of the slide table is best checked by the same means as that used for checking the squareness of a drilling machine table ; most readers will be familiar with this, but for the benefit of those who are not, here it is.

Mount a scriber point in the lathe in such a way that it can be made to describe a circle practically equal in diameter to the width of the slide table. A simple way of doing this is to take the scriber and clamp block of an ordinary surface gauge and attach it to a piece of steel bar the same diameter as the pillar of the gauge, held in the lathe chuck. The distance between the scriber point and the slide table should be the same at all points of rotation if the slide is accurate and properly set up all ways.

Should any error be apparent when this test is made, do not hesitate, or consider it *infra dig*, to adjust matters with a slip of thin packing—metal, fibre or even paper—under the foot of the slide ; it is a much quicker and more effective remedy than reviling the makers of the vertical slide, or sending the offending components to them for correction.

Squaring and Levelling

The squareness of the slide is sometimes tested by means of a try-square set on the lathe bed, but this assumes that the latter is truly parallel with the axis of the lathe mandrel, which is not always correct. A square may be used for checking the vertical accuracy of the side edge of the slide table, however, and is useful when setting a swivelling slide to the perpendicular position. A scribing block may be used for checking horizontal accuracy of work held on the slide, and if the scriber point is set exactly to centre height, will serve for centring the work for end milling.

The use of the vertical slide for carrying dividing attachments or milling spindles will be dealt with in the sections referring to these appliances.

All the milling operations so far described have been carried out by using the lathe mandrel as the cutter spindle, and the lathe slide-rest, or attachments mounted thereon, as a means of holding the work. Generally speaking, this method is the most efficient, particularly for the heavier classes of work, because the lathe mandrel is well adapted to withstand the stresses imposed in milling, and can also transmit a fair amount of power, at speeds varying over a wide range, without involving any difficulties or complications in the way of driving gear.

CHAPTER V

ROTARY SPINDLE ATTACHMENTS

O CCASIONS arise where it is more convenient to hold the work in the lathe chuck, or between centres, and carry the cutter on an auxiliary spindle mounted on the slide-rest. This method is particularly applicable in such operations as gear-cutting, or other work involving indexing, and one of its practical advantages in this case is that gear blanks or similar components, which have been turned in the lathe, may be milled at the same setting, thus eliminating any possible risk of concentric inaccuracy in the milling. In some cases, rotary-spindle milling attachments may be used on work which is not carried on the lathe mandrel. This, again, permits of two alternatives ; either the work may be mounted on the lathe bed, and the cutter spindle on the slide-rest, or *vice versa*.

Some forms of rotary-spindle milling attachments are designed to mount on the top-slide of the lathe, or on the vertical slide (according to whether or not vertical adjustment is necessary for a particular operation) while others, of more elaborate design, are equipped with a mounting which incorporates elevating gear. It is not possible to say offhand which is the more desirable ; much depends on individual details of design and construction, but it is reasonable to expect that a mounting designed expressly for the purpose of carrying the cutter spindle may be better adapted to this purpose than a vertical slide, which must cope with a wide variety of duties, and thus embody features which represent a compromise between various incompatible factors in design.

Simple Cutter Frames

The simplest form of rotary-spindle appliance is the " cutter frame," which is an inheritance from horological practice, and is quite useful for light work, such as the cutting of small spur wheels and pinions for instruments. In its original and primitive form, the spindle is mounted in centre-point bearings, and is designed primarily to carry single-point fly-cutters, though in any case it may be adapted to use multi-toothed cutters, which are much to be preferred when working in steel or other hard metals. Such cutters, however, are liable to call for more power than fly-cutters, and may have to be run at lower speed, so that a speed-reducing gear must be fitted to the cutter frame. Then the load on the bearings increases so that the primitive form of bearings cannot cope with it adequately, and it becomes necessary to design a more substantial bearing.

It will, therefore, be seen that the simple cutter frame, when applied to a heavier class of work than that encountered by the horologist, is liable to evolve into a much heavier and more elaborate device ; but in some cases this policy has been carried to extremes, so as to produce a clumsy and cumbersome appliance which may possibly have greater rigidity and power capacity, but is much less handy and adaptable than the primitive form of frame.

The cutter frame illustrated in Figs. 34 and 35 is primarily intended to be carried in the tool-post of the lathe. It is equipped with a worm gear drive giving a reduction of 9 to 1, and is adapted to take small milling cutters of standard type. The frame may be cut or forged from solid mild steel, or cast in good quality iron, and unless it is intended to be used permanently in the vertical position, the mounting shank must be provided with means to allow swivelling movement. As shown, the shank is flattened for clamping in the tool-post, and the other end is turned to fit a hole in the frame, where it is secured by a lock nut on the inner

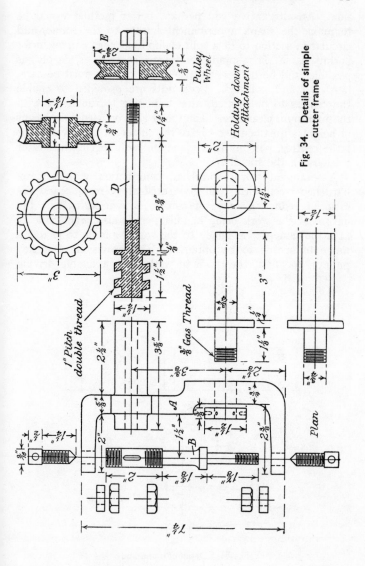

Fig. 34. Details of simple cutter frame

side.   An alternative and perhaps better method would be
to make the shank a permanent fixture to the frame, and
circular in section to fit a split clamp holder, as employed for
boring bars.   The spindle ends are centred as deeply as
possible, and both these and the point centres must be case-
hardened and polished.   Lock nuts are provided to enable
the centres to be secured, after adjusting to run freely with
the minimum clearance.   They may also be used as a means
of height adjustment, to centre the cutter on the level of the
lathe centres, possibly in conjunction with spacing bushes or
washers on the spindle.

A gunmetal worm wheel, in conjunction with a case-
hardened steel worm, will give satisfactory results, and the
ratio of reduction may, of course, be varied to suit the
nature of the work being handled ; it is also practicable to
fit a multi-step cone pulley to the worm spindle to enable a
range of speeds to be obtained.   The provision of jockey
pulleys, to adapt the drive to work from available driving

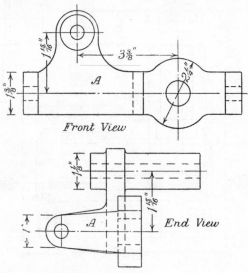

Fig. 35.   Detail of frame body

gear, is often necessary, and a convenient way of mounting the jockey spindle is on a bracket clamped to the boss of the worm shaft bearing. (This matter is discussed more fully in the section dealing with the means of driving cutter spindles.)

When using a cutter frame of this type to cut small gears, it is usual to mount it with the spindle axis vertical, and the cutter centre level with the lathe centres, so that it cuts horizontally across the front side of the gear blank. For feeding towards the chuck, the spindle should run anti-clockwise, viewed from above. Many other positions and arrangements of the frame, however, are possible, and may be exploited with advantage in dealing with various milling problems. Spur or bevel reduction gearing is sometimes used as an alternative to the worm gearing, but does not permit of such a large ratio of reduction in a single stage. Another advantage of worm gearing is that it enables different gear ratios to be obtained with little or no alteration of gear centres.

The photograph on page 45 shows simple cutter frames used by Mr. K. N. Harris, the one on the right having a plain, direct driven spindle, intended only to carry fly-cutters, and provided with a jockey pulley bracket. The frame on the left is equipped with worm reduction gearing, and the spindle takes multi-toothed milling cutters. A lug is provided on this frame, with a hole to fit the tool-post stud, whereas the other frame has a square shank to clamp in the ordinary way.

A Correction

It may be noticed that in the drawings of the simple cutter frame (Fig. 34), the collar on the cutter spindle prevents assembly of the lower location-adjusting nut for the worm wheel, but a slight modification to the spindle would enable it to be corrected. The collar could be made loose, or its diameter reduced to the core size of the threaded part, so that the nut would slip over it. Adjusting nuts above and below the worm wheel are desirable, to enable it to be centred accurately in relation to the worm, without affecting the height of the cutter or the setting of the pivot screws ; but the design of this simple appliance will probably be modified, in any case, to suit the requirements of individual constructors.

Milling and Drilling Spindles

The provision of a really substantial bearing, with adequate lubrication, is a great advantage, especially when the spindle is subjected to frequent or continuous running under heavy load. It is, of course, possible to provide the simple cutter frame with improved bearings. Sometimes this is done by making the spindle hollow, and running it on a long bolt passing right through between the horns of the frame. Generally, however, it is better to extend the spindle and run it in bearings carried in the horns of the frame ; these usually have to be of the split " plummer block " type, in order to allow of removing the spindle for fitting the cutter in position.

In recent years, a form of cutter spindle, having a long bearing in the centre, and with the cutter fitted at one extremity, and the pulley or gearing at the other, has become extremely popular. Appliances of this nature are usually termed " milling and drilling spindles," because the open-ended spindle obviously provides facilities for using it to carry drills—also, incidentally, end mills, which cannot be used in the ordinary cutter frame. If the bearings of the appliance are well designed, this form of device works extremely well, and may be equipped with a hollow spindle with a Morse taper socket to carry taper shank drills and cutters, or bored for standard split collets.

A very simple milling and drilling spindle, having provision for either direct drive or spur reduction gearing, is illustrated in Fig. 36. It has a plain socket to take $\frac{1}{2}$-in. shanks, secured by a grub screw, but may obviously be adapted to take other methods of fitting. If desired, the lug which carries the spindle for the reduction gear pinion may be extended and slotted to allow of mesh adjustment for gears of different sizes, so that the lathe change wheels may be used, in various combinations, to produce the required reduction ratio.

The body of the appliance may conveniently be made from

a casting in iron or good quality gunmetal, which will provide quite a good bearing for the steel spindle, without bushing, provided that it is bored to a really good fit throughout its length, and is kept well lubricated. It is an advantage to "chamber out" the centre of the bore, or slightly reduce the diameter of the shaft, to leave an annular space which serves as a reserve oil well, and helps to keep up continuous lubrication on runs of long duration.

Another simple milling and drilling spindle is illustrated in Fig. 37. The body of this appliance is made of square section mild steel, and it is, therefore, advisable to fit bronze bushes for the bearings at either end. A three-speed cone pulley is fitted to the spindle, which is hollow, and provided with a taper socket, also a ball thrust race. End play is taken up by adjusting and locking collars at the pulley end. This type of spindle demands very careful workmanship if its potential advantages are to be realised, and the spindle may with advantage, be hardened and ground on all working surfaces; but if these conditions are observed, it will give excellent service.

One disadvantage in this and also the preceding type

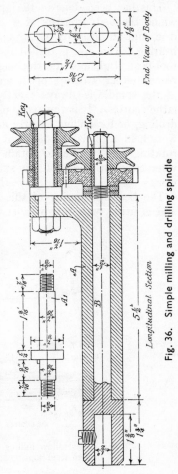

Fig. 36.   Simple milling and drilling spindle

of appliance, both of which are designed so that the bearing housing is clamped in the tool-post, is that the latter may become distorted by the clamping pressure, and thus bind on the shaft. To avoid this, it is better to provide a lug or other extension which will take the strain of clamping, leaving the bearing quite free.

This has been done in the appliance shown in Fig. 38, in which the body consists of a casting having a solid central disc, and an offset barrel, which is bored to take the spindle bearing. The disc is drilled in the centre to drop over the tool-post stud, and its thickness is adjusted so that when placed either way up, or in any angular position, the axis of the spindle is always exactly at the same height as the lathe centres. It is thus very useful for diametral or angular drilling, or for milling exactly across the centre of a piece of work held in the lathe chuck ; it may also be used as a contra-rotating drill spindle, to obtain the effect of increased speed when concentric holes of very small size are required in turned work.

The bearing housing of this appliance is unusually long, and is fitted with two parallel Oilite self-lubricating bushes,

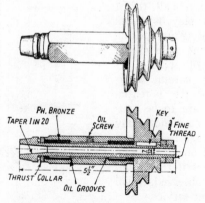

Fig. 37. Hollow milling spindle with bronze-bushed steel housing and ball thrust race

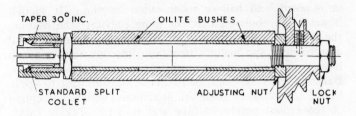

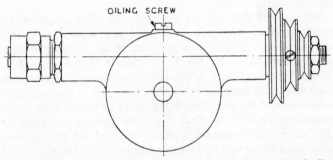

Fig. 38. Milling and drilling spindle with push-in collet chuck and offset clamping pad

with a large oil reservoir in the centre. A simple collet chuck of the " push-in " type is fitted, the end of the spindle being screwed with a fine thread to take the cap of the chuck, and the taper socket for the collets was bored while the spindle was running in its own bearings.

One purpose for which this spindle was specially intended was for the drilling of a number of holes equally spaced around a circle, as, for instance, a bolting flange or indexing plate, and it has proved extremely useful for this purpose, but it is also applicable to any milling or drilling work within the capacity of a directly-driven spindle in this class.

There is scope for design in the bearings of milling and drilling spindles, and many of these have been fitted with contractible tapered bushes, also double cone bearings, single or opposed, and ball or roller radial bearings. It should, however, be observed that the more elaborate the bearing, the more meticulous must be its accuracy of construction and adjustment ; and many attempts to improve bearing design have been abortive because of deficiencies in these respects. Ball and roller bearings, in particular, are difficult to apply to real advantage on these simple spindles, with the exception of those used purely to take end thrust.   Taking things by and large, the constructor of such an appliance will find that a really well-fitted parallel spindle is hard to beat for general work.

Milling and drilling spindles equipped with special slides and mounting standards may be found advantageous for certain classes of work.   A very ingenious example of such an appliance made by Mr. K. N. Harris, for use on a 4-in. James Spencer lathe, is illustrated in the photographs on page 49.   It is designed to fit the cross-slide of the lathe, the base flange of the standard being made to match that of the swivelling top-slide, so that it fits the seating provided for the latter.   A horizontal slide is provided for the spindle, with sensitive lever feed, and an adjustable travel-limiting stop.   The driving pulley may be attached directly to the spindle, or it may operate through the spur reduction gearing, which, as seen in the photographs, is completely enclosed in a casing which clamps on the spindle-bearing housing. Lubricators are provided for both the spindle and the gear-shaft bearings, and a collet chuck is fitted to the spindle to carry drills or milling cutters.

The utility of the horizontal slide and sensitive feed on this appliance is found mainly in connection with fine drilling ; for milling, the slide can be locked, and feed applied by using the longitudinal and cross-slide adjustments of the lathe.

The Potts Milling Appliances

One of the best known commercially-made rotary spindle appliances at present on the market is that made by Mr. G. P. Potts, of Ruthin Road, Denbigh, North Wales, and is illustrated on page 50. The utility of this device, which is extremely well made and finished, though moderate in cost, can be attested to by many readers of *The Model Engineer*. It embodies a hollow spindle, running in closely-fitted bronze bushes, with adjusting and locking collars to take up end play, and a two-step cone pulley for vee belt keyed on the end. The nose of the spindle may be supplied bored to take either No. 1 Morse taper or " A " size collets.

In order to enable the height of the spindle to be adjusted, the spindle housing is attached to the sole-plate by a pivot bolt, which allows it to be swung up or down in an arc around the bolt centre, so that when clamped on the top slide by the tool-post stud, a sufficiently wide range of elevation adjustment may be obtained for most ordinary purposes. It is, however, practicable to increase this range by mounting the complete appliance on a vertical slide, as will be seen later. For lathes which have different forms of tool-post fittings, other than the single stud type, it is possible to adapt the Potts spindle by modifying the mounting bracket or sole-plate, and it is shown on pages 67 and 68, suited to the $3\frac{1}{2}$-in. Drummond or Myford " M " type lathe, which has a large diameter cast pillar on the top-slide for the attachment of the tool-post. In this case, a split clamp is provided to mount the milling spindle.

This photograph also shows how jockey pulleys may be supported from the spindle housing, to enable alignment errors in the driving belt to be corrected, or to change the angle of drive. The arm on which the jockey pulley shaft is mounted is pivotally attached to the lug of a split clamp which embraces the spindle housing. Jockey pulley fittings are not included with the standard equipment of the appliance, but are obtainable as extras.

Vertical-Column Milling Attachments

Another useful milling attachment made by Mr. Potts, embodying a spindle similar in general essentials to that described above, is illustrated in the next photograph. This type of appliance is representative of a class of " vertical column " milling attachments which have been very popular in the past, and have been made in various forms, with minor variations in detail design or equipment, by amateur constructors. It may be said that the Potts attachment embodies all the essential features of its type, and in common with the milling spindle described, is very well made and fitted.

The hollow vertical column which forms the main slide is rotatably mounted by a long centre stud, on a flat baseplate flange, which can be shaped and drilled to mount on the cross-slide of the lathe. On most British lathes, a plain rectangular base, with two bolt holes or slots positioned to match the tee-slots in the cross-slide, will fill all requirements ; but on some foreign lathes, which do not have the tee-slotted table on the cross-slide, a special form of base may be necessary. The sliding bracket is split for fit adjustment or clamping on the pillar, and has a tapped lug which forms the lead-screw nut. A key fitted to the bore of the bracket, and sliding in a keyway running the full length of the pillar, maintains alignment of the vertical traversing movement.

The spindle housing is mounted on the sliding bracket by means of a pivot stud, which provides swivelling movement of the spindle to any angle, and a graduated protractor is provided on the seating flange. It will be seen that this movement, in conjunction with the rotatable movement of the pillar, provides " universal " or " spherical " angular adjustment of the spindle.

It may be observed that some attachments of the vertical-column type have been found to lack rigidity, owing to weakness of the column, the bracket, or the means of preventing the latter from rotating on the column. The use of a sliding key, of limited size, to take heavy torque stresses in the slides of machine tools, is a feature which has often been strongly criticised as inherently unsound, but a great deal depends on details of design, and even more on the way they are carried out. A column of prismatic form would probably be more rigid against torque stresses ; but it would also be much more expensive and difficult, both to machine and fit, than the round column, which accounts for the popularity of the latter in milling attachments employed in amateur workshops.

Mr. Bradley's adaptation of the Potts spindle for use on vertical slide

The Potts grindi
spindle

The " Abwood "
vertical milling
attachment

Application of " dwarf " overhead gear for driving vertical cutter spindle

Simple plain-bearing milling spindle for use on the vertical slide

The plug mandrel shown in Fig. 49, and the spring plunger shown in Fig. 50, in use on a Myford ML4 lathe

Cutting a spur gear with a milling spindle mounted on the vertical slide

90

Milling Spindle Arrangements

Some highly ingenious and practical applications of the Potts milling spindle have been devised by Mr. Ian Bradley. These have already been described by him in *The Model Engineer*, but in view of the way in which they demonstrate essential principles, it is hoped that no apology will be necessary for bringing them once more to the notice of readers. Mr. Bradley uses the simple form of the Potts milling spindle, mounted on a standard Senior non-swivelling vertical slide, for examples of operations illustrated on page 87. It will be seen that the range and adaptability of the equipment are further extended by the use of a slotted plate of mild steel, introduced between the sole-plate of the milling spindle and the table of the vertical slide. The gear wheel seen in the photographs on pages 70 and 87, is simply a scrap component, utilised as a parallel distance piece to increase the effective range of overhang in front of the vertical slide. A very neat form of jockey pulley mounting will be observed, consisting of a split clamp on the spindle housing, with a long stalk attached, on which is clamped a vertical pillar carrying the jockey pulley shaft.

The first example shows the assembly mounted on the cross-slide of the lathe, with the spindle vertical, so that it can be used for vertical milling operations on work held in the lathe chuck ; in the particular case shown, it is cutting a keyway in a shaft. As already described, this operation can be done without a rotary-spindle appliance, by running the cutter in the lathe chuck and mounting the work on the cross-slide, but the particular advantage of a vertical spindle is that it facilitates observation of the work, and in many cases simplifies setting up and holding, especially if it is desired to make angular or indexing adjustments round the work centre.

It will readily be seen that with the assembly set up as shown, milling could be carried out on a piece of work mounted rigidly on the lathe bed, as the longitudinal, cross, and vertical adjustments are all available for moving the cutter spindle. Automatic traversing feeds, as provided on the lathe, are also available for feeding the cutter.

In the second example, the assembly is mounted on a parallel packing block on the lathe bed, to the right (*i.e.* tail-stock side) of the saddle, in which position it is available for vertical milling of work clamped to the cross-slide, as shown. The driving arrangements are exactly as before, and again, any automatic feeds with which the lathe may be equipped, are available. In both these examples, the spindle is not restricted to the vertical position but may be set at any angle, or even in the horizontal position, if desired.

The third example on page 69, shows the assembly again mounted on the cross-slide, but in this case it is arranged for dealing with a heavier milling operation—namely, spur gear cutting—for which a reduction gearing in the spindle drive is desirable. This is provided in a very ingenious manner, by pressing into service the components of a small hand drill, including the bevel gears, which are in this case used in the reverse way to that originally intended, that is, to obtain a reduction instead of an increase of speed. The drill frame, with its spindle and bevel pinion, is mounted on the jockey pulley arm, and the crown wheel, by means of a suitable adaptor, is attached to the milling spindle. No alteration is made to the jockey pulley fittings, but the spindle is underslung from the arm to suit the particular driving arrangements employed.

The milling cutter is carried on an arbor which fits the socket of the spindle, and in order to support the lower end of the arbor, an outrigger bearing is arranged, in an arm bolted to the rear end of the cross-slide, alignment of this bearing being adjusted before final clamping down. As the cutter works at a fixed height for this operation, exactly level with the lathe centres, no working adjustment of the vertical slide is required, and once set, the slide gibs may be tightened up to prevent inadvertent movement. The outrigger bearing is equipped with a lubricator, and immediately above it, a conical collar is fitted to the arbor, to deflect swarf and dust which might otherwise get into the bearing.

Other forms of milling spindles or cutter frames may be adapted to work in similar ways to that shown here. To those readers who question the utility of lathe milling appliances, the quality of the work turned out by Mr. Bradley, and other model engineers who use these methods, should be a sufficient answer.

Mention has already been made of the many types of rotary spindle appliances which are, or have been, provided as special equipment for various makes of lathes. Generally speaking, these differ only in detail from the types of attachments which have been described here, and call for no special comment. The accessories for well-known types of horological or instrument lathes nearly always include milling spindles of some kind or other, and among manufacturers of lathes known to model engineers, Drummond, Milnes, and Britannia formerly listed special attachments of this type.

Grinding Spindles

Strictly speaking, these do not come within the scope of the present treatise, but as they have much in common with milling and drilling spindles, a passing mention of them may be justified. Some forms of milling spindles can be, and have been, used to carry internal or external grinding wheels but generally, it may be said that the special requirements of grinding spindles, namely, light and easy running bearings, with provision for running at very high speed, are not well catered for in the form of appliance best suited for milling purposes. The speed required for really efficient grinding with small diameter wheels may be of the order of 20,000 r.p.m., or even higher, which is not easily attained with the usual means available for driving these spindles, and there are many other special problems in the application of grinding processes to ordinary lathe work.

Mr. G. P. Potts manufactures a special grinding spindle for use in the lathe, having provision for carrying a wheel for external grinding at one end, and a socket, tapered for No. 1 Morse or " A " size collets at the other, to take an extension spindle for internal grinding wheels. As seen on page 88, the frame is adapted to clamp on the top-slide of the lathe by the usual single tool-post stud, and split bronze bearings are fitted, with adequate lubricators. This spindle runs very sweetly at high r.p.m., and is well balanced, so that no perceptible vibration can be detected.

Cam Generating with the Milling Spindle

An interesting application of a simple milling appliance for producing cam profiles of high precision was described some years ago in *The Model Engineer*, by Mr. D. H. Chaddock. The milling spindle in this case was made, or at least adapted, specially for the purpose, using a small headstock made from a lathe tailstock casting to house the spindle bearing at exactly the same height as the lathe centres, when mounted on the cross-slide. Any of the milling spindles described above, however, could be used, if mounted horizontally. The spindle nose was arranged to carry a single fly-cutter at an angle of 45 degrees, as in the example illustrated in Fig. 7, and functioned as a small face mill, operating on the cam blank held in the lathe chuck. To produce the correct cam profile, a combination of indexing movement of the lathe spindle, and cross movement of the slide, was employed, the exact lift of the cam at every angular position of rotation being previously worked out. In the event of the cross-slide not being fitted with a graduated index, or the precision of the latter being dubious, a dial test indicator could be used to check the increments of lift, by fixing it on the cross-slide, with the plunger in contact with a fixed abutment on the saddle, or *vice versa*.

Although not specifically mentioned by Mr. Chaddock, this method might be simply adapted to the production of cams or other profiles by a copying process. The master cam or template would have to be mounted concentrically with the blank (as by mounting both on a true-running mandrel), and a flat-faced contact follower mounted on the cross-slide. If the diameter of the copy is required to be exactly the same as the " master," it would be necessary to ensure that the distance of the follower from the lathe axis is exactly the same as that of the cutter point. Another necessary factor in producing an accurate copy is that the follower should be exactly the same shape on its face as the surface which would normally be produced by the cutter on stationary work, which in this case is flat. (See illustration, page 61.)

Should this method ever be used in conjunction with a cutter having its axis parallel to that of the work, i.e., cutting on the periphery, it would be necessary to use a follower in the form of a disc or arc of the same radius as that of the cutter. Unless these precautions are observed, small but possibly important discrepancies may be introduced in the accuracy of the copy.

With this method, exact accuracy in the indexing of the blank is of no importance; it is only necessary to shift it through a very small angle for each cut, and feed the cutter in until the follower makes contact with the master profile. It is even possible to arrange to keep the lathe mandrel in constant rotation at a very slow rate, and use a spring to keep the cross-slide pressed inwards to bring the follower in contact with the master profile ; the lead screw of the slide being, of course, temporarily disconnected. Exactly the same methods, by the way, can be used for cam or profile grinding in the lathe.

Vertical Milling Attachments

It has already been seen that the ordinary milling spindle can be used at various angles, including both horizontal and vertical positions. Some forms of milling attachments, however, have been designed for use mainly or exclusively in the vertical position, their object being to convert the lathe practically into a light vertical mill. One of the best known, produced some 20 years ago was the "Abwood" milling attachment illustrated on page 88. It embodied a rigid vertical bracket adapted to bolt on the lathe bed, in front of the headstock, and carrying a milling spindle on a slide which provided vertical adjustment. The drive to the spindle was taken, through bevel gears and a vertical shaft, from the lathe mandrel, so that a full range of speeds and ample power was available at the cutter spindle. While this device was undoubtedly sound in principle, and of great utility, it was apparently too elaborate and expensive for most users of small lathes, and, so far as can be gathered, did not attain any great popularity.

Another vertical milling attachment was made about the same time by the manufacturers of the once well-known Relmac lathe, and known as the " Relmil." In this case the milling spindle was carried on a round steel column mounted vertically at the back of the lathe bed, so that the lathe could be used for normal work with the attachment in position, and it could be brought into action on work mounted between the lathe centres, though in this case, its utility was limited by the lack of horizontal feed movements. A vertical slide was provided for the cutter spindle, which had a sliding key in the drive from the pulley, working at a fixed height in its own bearings, and driven from a special countershaft running along the back of the lathe. In this case also, no very great degree of popularity seems to have been attained by the appliance.

A somewhat similar arrangement to that of the Abwood attachment can be produced by mounting a small drilling machine on the bed of the lathe, and driving it, through the usual jockey pulleys, from a pulley held in the lathe chuck. The example on page 126 was used by Mr. D. H. Chaddock to deal with a special milling problem, for which purpose it was entirely successful. A machine of the " quill " spindle type is best suited for this work, and the bearings must be really well fitted ; some means of clamping the vertical adjustment is also essential. It would be very desirable to have some provision for fine adjustment, as by means of screw feed, but this is rarely fitted to small drilling machines of the type likely to be applicable. As a matter of fact, the usual small drilling machine spindle is not designed to deal with heavy side thrusts as encountered in milling, and for serious work of this nature, it would be best to design a special spindle, with bearings more suited to the purpose, and preferably socketed to take taper-shank cutters or collet chucks.

Stencil Milling

The particular operation for which this set-up was used by Mr. Chaddock was the milling of end-plates for a rotary blower, in which ribs were formed by milling away the major part of the surface, in other words, an " intaglio " process. To facilitate this work, the cutter was guided by means of a steel " stencil plate," having openings corresponding to the shape of the cut-away portion of the end-plate, to which it was bolted in the appropriate position. The form of cutter used was a two-bladed end mill, having cutting teeth formed only close to the end, so that when fed in to the correct depth, the portion of the cutter shank level with the guide plate acts simply as a locating pin or roller, limiting the traverse of the work by coming in contact with the plate, and enabling the contour of the latter to be followed without risk of error or over-run. For work of this nature it is advisable to have the work free to move in any direction, but at the same time fully under control, so that it may either be clamped to a base large enough for comfortable handling, which is laid on the cross-slide without bolting down, or it may be clamped to the cross-slide, and the lead screw of the latter removed.

The use of a stencil, template or guide-plate has become very popular in recent years for " routing " operations in the softer metals, using high-speed cutters, and it has been found to be one of the most expeditious methods of cutting out complicated shapes in light alloy, wood or plastics, to a high degree of accuracy and finish.

There are many other possibilities in the use of simple milling spindles on the lathe or other machine tools. They have been used with special feed or control devices for producing accurate two-dimensional or three-dimensional forms in die-sinking and other tool making operations. The well-known type of engraving machines which have now become almost indispensable in many departments of engineering practice, and are every day finding new applications, are simply high-speed milling spindles, with control by means of a pantograph, which enables them to reproduce the outline, and in some cases the relief, of a master profile to any desired scale.

A very interesting application of the reduced-scale copying principle is found in the medallion lathe, which is used for copying coins, medals, plaques and other low-relief sculptures on a reduced scale (Fig. 39). It comprises two headstocks with spindles and faceplates geared together to rotate at the same speed, and in the same direction. One of these carries the model or " master " and the other the blank to be engraved. At right angles to the axis of the spindles is arranged a rigid beam or lever, articulated to pivot in both the vertical and

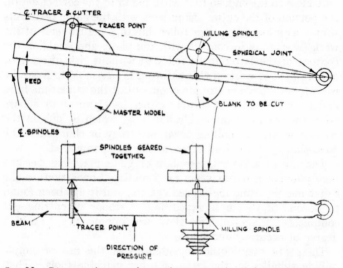

Fig. 39. Diagram showing the working principle of the medallion lathe

horizontal planes, by means of a spherical or double knuckle joint. On this is mounted a stylus or tracer point to make contact with the master, and a milling spindle with an end or point cutter to operate on the blank. The distances of the spindle and the stylus from the pivot must be in the ratio of scale reduction, i.e., for copying to one-eighth scale, the distance of the stylus from the pivot of the beam must be eight times that of the cutter point. The beam is pressed towards the master faceplate by means of a weight or spring, and with the spindles slowly rotating, it is swung gradually in the other plane to feed the stylus and cutter from the outer edge of their respective working circles to the centre. In this way the entire surface of the profile on the master plate is covered, and the form of the master is reproduced to scale on the blank. This method is used not only for direct copying of large models in comparatively soft metals, but also making dies in tool steel, from which coins, etc., are produced by stamping. The principles of this machine could be adapted to milling in the lathe.

Many ingenious applications of milling spindles were employed by the users of ornamental turning lathes, for such purposes as ornamenting wood or metal objects by the process known as " engine turning." This consisted in the turning of eccentric circles around the face or periphery of the work, indexing the latter to produce interlacing or overlapping geometric figures. An extraordinary amount of care, patience and ingenuity was devoted to this work, which largely has died out, except for examples which are perpetuated by the Worshipful Company of Turners, and exhibited at their exhibitions.

An application of the rotary spindle to what may be termed " Planetary " milling is not without interest, both from the ornamental and utility aspects. It consists in mounting a milling spindle eccentrically on the lathe face-plate, either parallel to the lathe axis, or at any other angle, and indexing it around the lathe axis either to produce geometric forms, or simply to provide a height adjustment to the milling cutter.

CHAPTER VI

MEANS OF DRIVING CUTTER SPINDLES

ONE of the disadvantages of the rotary-spindle type of milling attachment, as compared to the use of appliances which utilise the lathe mandrel as the cutter spindle, is that special means of driving the spindle must be provided. As the latter does not work in a fixed position, being set at various angles and locations to suit the nature of the work, and also subject to feeding and traversing motion in taking a cut, it is no easy problem to devise a really satisfactory form of drive which will cope with all emergencies.

The ideal cutter spindle drive would have to fulfil the following conditions : (1) apply a smooth torque to the spindle irrespective of its position or angle, without producing forces tending to vibrate the spindle or force it out of its set position ; (2) furnish a full range of speeds to suit all materials and all classes of work being milled ; (3) supply ample power (i.e. torque) to the spindle to enable cutters to be used at their full cutting capacity. It may be said at once that these conditions are rarely, if ever, satisfied in their entirety, but, nevertheless, there are several forms of drive which are very convenient in use, and give excellent results within their limitations. These may be classified as follows : (1) hand drive ; (2) belt drive ; (3) flexible shaft drive ; (4) " motorised " drive, either direct, or through gears, belt, or flexible shaft transmission.

Hand Drive

This is the simplest and most primitive form of drive, but it is, perhaps, the least hampered of all drives in respect of dealing with problems of spindle angle and location, and it enables ample torque to be applied to the spindle for most milling operations within the scope of this discussion, though at only a limited range of speed. It entails no more complication to the milling attachment than the provision of a crank handle to the end of the spindle, for providing cutter speeds up to about 120 r.p.m., which is sufficient for many milling operations with multi-toothed side cutters, on the harder metals, such as bronze, cast-iron, or steel, but is not high enough for end milling or fly-cutter operations, especially on the softer metals. Higher speeds might possibly be obtained with direct hand drive for short periods, but are likely to be tiring, and the risk of shifting or vibrating the cutter by snatchy movement is accentuated. It is, of course, quite practicable to fit some kind of gearing to the spindle to enable the speed of the hand drive to be multiplied, but so far as experience goes, this is rarely done.

Certain positions of the spindle may be rather awkward for the application of hand drive, but generally speaking, it is as near universal in this respect as any form of drive can be.

While it is possible to adapt nearly any kind of milling spindle, with the exception of that used between centres in a cutter frame, to direct hand drive, it is generally advisable to construct a special spindle, having particularly long steady bearings, and an extension of the spindle, so as to carry the hand crank well clear of any projecting lathe fittings. This makes for comfortable handling and avoids the risk of damage to the knuckles in turning the crank.

A very simple form of hand milling spindle is illustrated in Fig. 40, applied to a spur gear cutting operation in the lathe. It will be seen that the bearing housing of the spindle is adapted to be clamped in the tool-post, being in the form of a square bar drilled through the centre and bushed at each end, similar to some of the devices previously described. The effective length of bearing must be sufficient to minimise the risk of springing or shifting the cutter by inadvertent side pressure applied when turning the crank, and the extension of the spindle beyond the bearing should not be carried to extremes, owing to the side leverage which may be exerted on a long projecting shaft.

In the example shown, no provision is made for height adjustment of the milling spindle, and packing would have to be used under the shank to bring the cutter to the required height. It is, of course, practicable to mount the appliance on a vertical slide to provide height adjustment, but in cases where the latter is not available, a simple means of height adjustment may be provided on the spindle itself.

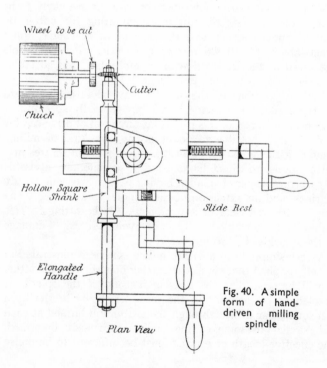

Fig. 40. A simple form of hand-driven milling spindle

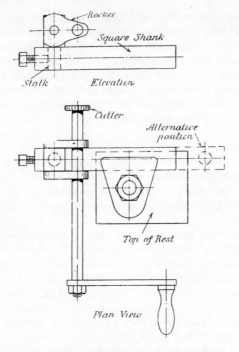

Fig. 41. Hand-driven spindle with rocking adjustment for height

The spindle illustrated in Fig. 41 has a rocking adjustment to the bearing, which in this case consists of a long tube, extending right from the cutter to the web of the crank handle, and preferably bushed at each end. Two lugs are attached to the tube by brazing or welding, and these straddle a trunnion block which may either be an integral part of the mounting shank or mounted on it, with a choice of two or more positions, as shown. The height adjustment may be locked by tightening the trunnion bolt, or a further refinement may be provided. in the way of an elevating screw adjustment, if desired.

The most serious practical limitation of hand milling drive is the difficulty of turning the spindle evenly and smoothly, without introducing side thrust, while at the same time manipulating one or more slide-rest adjustments at an equally smooth rate. It is consequently rather difficult to ensure accuracy and good finish by this method, but, nevertheless, some very useful work has been produced by its aid in the hands of painstaking operators.

Belt Drive

This method of drive, in some form or other, is by far the most popular for driving cutter spindles in the lathe, despite the problems which it involves in applying the drive at odd angles, and the limitations in torque or range of speed which it imposes.

It is necessary to provide, not only for reasonable alignment of the belt, but also for alteration of the distance between driving pulleys, which would affect belt tension, in the absence of some means to take up slack in the drive. For the first, it may be said that the use of round belts, in grooved pulleys having a vee angle of about 60 degrees, and ample depth of groove, provide a fair latitude in respect of alignment, but it is necessary to use guide or " jockey " pulleys to enable drives to be taken at appreciably different angles. Belt tension is usually compensated by means of jockey pulleys on a slide, beam or lever loaded by means of a weight or spring.

Overhead Gear

The most popular form of belt driving device for milling spindles is the well-known " overhead gear," which has been fitted to many types of instrument or ornamental lathes as a standard accessory. It consists essentially of a special countershaft adapted to the required purpose, situated at a sufficient height above the lathe bed to enable an efficient belt drive to be provided to the cutter spindle, and to avoid any interference with the normal operation of the lathe. Belt tensioning gear is usually provided. In treadle lathes, the countershaft is driven from the treadle shaft or foot motor by a long belt, the normal lathe belt being removed, as it is not required when milling operations are in progress (see Fig. 42). Power-driven lathes may have the overhead gear driven from the standard countershaft, or direct from the driving motor. In some cases, the normal power countershaft can be adapted to serve as the overhead gear shaft, but this may impose limitations which are undesirable.

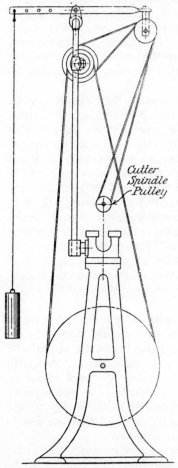

*Cutter
Spindle
Pulley*

The arrangement of overhead gear shown in Fig. 42 is a very common one, and it will be seen that the entire equipment is carried on a vertical frame attached to the back of the lathe bed. In some respects, this is open to criticism, as any vibration produced by the gearing is transmitted directly to the lathe, but it has been used with success for many years by innumerable operators. Mounting the frame or standards from the lower part of the lathe stand, or on an entirely separate foundation, may, however, be a very practical improvement.

Fig. 42. Arrangement of overhead gear commonly used for treadle lathe

To provide a range of speeds, it is usual to

fit a cone pulley on the overhead shaft, having steps to correspond with those on the lathe mandrel (though not necessarily the same size), to take the drive from the treadle wheel ; these, of course, may be either flat or grooved, according to the type of lathe drive employed. Another cone pulley may be employed to take the drive to the cutter spindle, in this case grooved for a round belt, of a suitable size to transmit the torque required, while at the same time sufficiently flexible to run freely in a path which may, on occasion, be very tortuous.

The method of maintaining constant belt tension will be clearly seen from this illustration. It consists of a beam mounted at the top of the frame, having at one end a bracket for the jockey pulley shaft, and at the other a weight hanger. Two grooved jockey pulleys are used, each running freely and independently on the shaft, as they will have to rotate in opposite directions when in use. It will be seen that the effect of the weight on the rear end of the beam will be to keep the jockey pulleys strained upwards, thereby maintaining practically constant tension of the belt, at all elevations or cross positions of the spindle. The counterweight may be varied in weight, or its leverage altered by hanging it at different distances from the pivot of the beam, to produce the belt tension desired ; in some cases, the weight is substituted by a spring.

To allow for variations of the lateral position of the cutter spindle along the lathe bed, the usual method is to make the spindle drive pulley adjustable along the overhead shaft, or in some cases a roller is fitted, on which the belt can align itself ; but in this case the advantage of speed variation, provided by a stepped pulley, is absent. The jockey pulley beam is also made laterally adjustable, or the jockey pulleys may be mounted on a long shaft, on which they are free to float endwise and find their own alignment.

This form of overhead gear allows of using the cutter spindle horizontally, at any angle from that parallel to the lathe axis, as shown, to the cross position, provided that the position of the jockey pulleys enables something like correct

Simple indexing device and vertical slide, as formerly supplied for use on the 4-in. Drummond round-bed lathe

Facing a heavy casting with a fly-cutter mounted on the faceplate

A division plate and index fitted to a plain lathe

A worm-geared swivelling dividing head with collet chuck, steady bar and back centre

The " Biflex " flexible-shaft driving unit

Belt tensioning device fitted to countershaft, as in Fig. 44

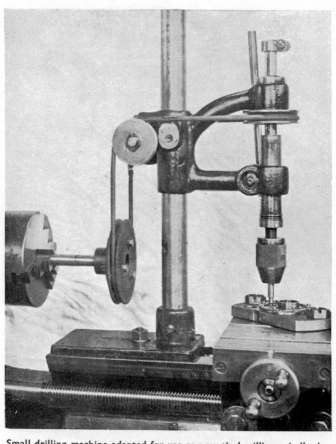

Small drilling machine adapted for use as a vertical milling spindle, by
Mr. D. H. Chaddock

alignment of the belt to be obtained. It may be found desirable to provide means of adjusting the jockey pulley shaft along the beam, but swivelling adjustment of this shaft is rarely of any advantage. For other positions of the cutter spindle than horizontal, it is necessary to use another pair of jockey pulleys to change the angle of the belt from the near-vertical plane to the required horizontal or angular plane. These pulleys may be mounted on a bracket carried by the spindle housing, as described in dealing with rotary-spindle appliances.

Many variations of the overhead gear shown are possible, one of them being known as the " dwarf " overhead gear, in which the need for the standards and countershaft is eliminated, drive being taken direct from the treadle, through jockey pulleys mounted on brackets attached to the lathe bed. While these variations may offer advantages for certain applications, they are not so universally adaptable as the standard form of overhead gear, and are comparatively little used.

Construction of Overhead Gear

A simple form of the overhead gear shown in Fig. 42, which is suitable for use on most small lathes, is illustrated in Fig. 43. The framework is intended to be made from steel tubing, ordinary gas, water or steam pipe, with standard screwed fittings, being suitable, though in modern practice welded joints are just as easy to carry out, and will probably work out just as cheaply, or more so. The dimensions given will suit lathes up to about $4\frac{1}{2}$-in. centres, and while it might be desirable to carry the overhead shaft at a greater height, to enable the length of cutter drive belt to be increased, thereby improving the driving efficiency and increasing latitude in belt alignment and tension, this makes manipulation of the belt more difficult, and may be impracticable in workshops with low head room.

The form of bearings shown for the overhead countershaft is perhaps the simplest it is possible to fit, consisting of hardened and pointed bolts which engage in deep centres in the end of the shaft. This form of bearing was once very popular for treadle shafts and other purposes in light machine-tool practice, and can be made to run very smoothly, with little friction, if carefully fitted and well lubricated. It is not, however, well suited to continuous running, and some constructors may prefer to keep more in touch with modern practice by running the shaft in ball races or self-aligning plain bearings. The former call for large diameter housings, which may be in the form of castings, bored to fit the races, at right-angles to the socket which is attached to the standard. Unless races of the self-aligning type are fitted, the housings must be very carefully lined up, by using a straight mandrel of the correct size fitted through the bores of both housings during assembly. Plain bearings may be found easier to fit, and run very smoothly if properly fitted, besides being quieter than ball bearings. Either gunmetal or cast-iron bushes will give excellent service for this class of duty, if regular but sparing lubrication is supplied.

The left-hand cone pulley should take the size and type of belt used for driving the lathe mandrel, and line up with the treadle pulley, the size of the steps being adjusted to provide constant belt tension at the different speeds. Means should be provided for shifting the other cone pulley along the shaft, a readily accessible set-screw being the simplest method of fixing ; the bracket for the jockey pulley beam should be similarly adjustable on the top tube of the frame. The brackets to carry the feet of the vertical tubes may be modified to suit the method of mounting, either by attachment to the lathe bed, or any other method which may be adopted. Cross-bracing of the frame may be found desirable to promote rigidity, and is easily carried out by bolting diagonal strips of about $\frac{1}{2}$-in. $\times$ $\frac{1}{4}$-in. flat steel across the space below the overhead shaft.

Although the jockey pulleys are shown as having vee grooves, it will be found that semi-circular grooves produce less friction, and work best under conditions of misalignment.

A typical example of the form of overhead gear supplied by lathe manufacturers as accessory equipment for the lathe

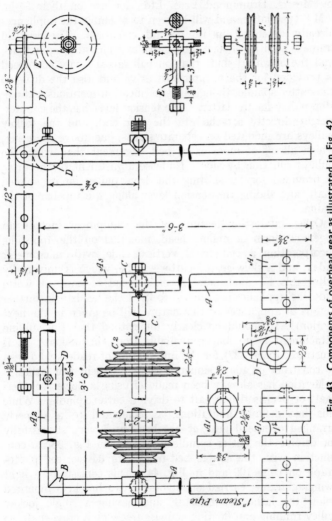

Fig. 43. Components of overhead gear as illustrated in Fig. 42

is shown on page 127. This attachment was formerly produced by Messrs. Drummond Bros. Ltd., for use on their 3½-in. " M " type lathe, and will be seen to resemble the appliances already described in its general essentials. The vertical frame is built up of steel tubes, with cast lugs at the junctions, and the overhead shaft runs on ball races. Only one speed is provided for the countershaft drive and also the drive to the cutter spindle, though the specification mentions a three-step pulley for the latter. The tension lever has the counter-weight directly attached to the rear end, and the jockey pulleys are mounted on separate shafts, one above the other, which allows of more exact belt alignment than when the pulleys run side by side. Endwise adjustment of the drive is provided for by shifting the drive pulley on its splined shaft, and sliding the tension lever along the top bar of the frame.

Other interesting features of this equipment include an ingenious form of milling head, mounted on the top-slide, incorporating a cylindrical vertical slide, with micrometer index, and a skew-geared cutter spindle, which is universally adjustable for angle, and reversible end to end. A worm indexing appliance is attached to the lathe headstock (further details of appliances of this nature will be given in the next section). It should be clearly understood that this milling attachment is no longer available from the makers ; it is illustrated (page 127), for the information of readers who wish to construct or adapt similar fittings for their own lathes.

Mention has already been made of using a power counter-shaft or overhead lineshaft to drive a cutter spindle. While this has definite limitations, as compared to a properly arranged overhead gear, it has been used very successfully for driving the cutter spindle illustrated in Fig. 38, in con-junction with the simple belt-tensioning device, see photo-graph on page 109 and in Fig. 44. This consists of a light swinging frame, carried on pivots in two brackets mounted below the lathe countershaft, and having a single jockey pulley running and floating endwise freely on a cross shaft, so that it can find its own alignment with the drive pulley, which may be shifted on the countershaft, and locked in any position with a set-screw. A long tension spring, anchored below the bracket, maintains an upward pressure on the jockey pulley.

This arrangement of the jockey pulley is only suitable for use with large diameter driving pulleys, and at best can only take up a limited amount of slack in the belt. It will, however, cope with a cross-traversing movement of the cutter spindle sufficient for most of the usual milling operations

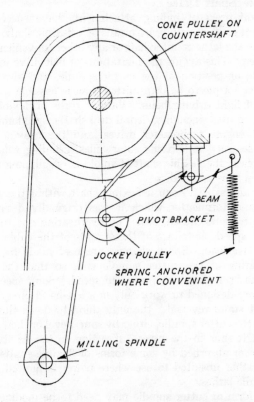

CONE PULLEY ON COUNTERSHAFT

BEAM

PIVOT BRACKET

JOCKEY PULLEY

SPRING ANCHORED WHERE CONVENIENT

MILLING SPINDLE

Fig. 44. Simple belt tensioning device for driving cutter spindle from power countershaft

dealt with in a small lathe. By using a doubled-back belt arrangement over two jockey pulleys, a considerable variation of belt length can be compensated, but it should be remembered that even with almost frictionless jockey pulleys, a good deal of power is absorbed in bending the belt over them. The simplest pulley arrangement is always the most efficient, and is recommended particularly where driving power is limited.

Flexible Shaft Drive

Several users of milling attachments have succeeded in driving them successfully by means of a flexible shaft, coupled either to the lathe countershaft or any other convenient source of power. This avoids the limitations of belt drive in respect of angle or position of the cutter spindle, and also enables a greater torque to be transmitted than is possible with most forms of light driving belts. Various types of flexible shafts have been used, including dental drill shafts, speedometer and aircraft engine tachometer drives, and the heavier flexible shafts designed for driving rotary files, grinding wheels, etc. In one case, the flexible shaft of an old horse-clipping machine has been thus adapted.

It is advisable to run a flexible shaft within the range of speed and torque for which it was originally designed, or trouble may be caused, either by overheating due to friction at high speed, or failure of the strands of the cable through torque overload. Speed changes are best made by altering the gearing at the cutter spindle end, so that the flexible shaft may run always at a constant speed. Some speedometer drives are designed to work only in a left-hand direction, and will not stand reversal ; the only thing to do in this case is to gear the cutter spindle, either by spur, bevel or skew gearing, so that it runs in the reverse direction to the flexible shaft. The power absorbed by some forms of flexible shafts renders them rather unsuited to use where power is limited, such as on treadle lathes.

The form of cutter spindle may need to be modified where flexible shaft drive is used. In most cases the shaft coupling is enclosed within a kind of union joint, so that when the outer cable is connected to the housing of the driven member, the inner shaft is automatically coupled by a square and socket, or spline. Similar arrangements are also provided at the other end of the shaft. It is often possible to adapt the driving gear of a speedometer, consisting of an enclosed right-angle skew or bevel gearing, to transmit the drive from the lineshaft or countershaft.

An example of a flexible-shaft appliance which can be adapted for milling in the lathe is the " Morrisflex " equipment illustrated on page 109. This is manufactured by Messrs. B. O. Morris Ltd., and comprises a portable driving motor, with flexible shaft, and a handpiece with chuck to hold rotary files and cutters. The latter can be adapted for mounting on the lathe tool-post or vertical slide to serve as a cutter spindle. In the particular appliance illustrated, known as the " Biflex," a 1/3 h.p. motor is provided, and this will furnish ample power for any operation likely to be encountered in the amateur workshop. Strictly speaking, a self-contained power unit of this nature should be classed under the heading of " motorised " attachments, to be described below.

" Motorised " Drive

The attachment of an electric motor directly to the milling appliance is quite a practical proposition, though it does not appear to have yet been done, so far as can be ascertained. It is, however, very common in modern grinding attachments, and very compact and powerful electric motors have been developed for this purpose. Such a motor, permanently attached and suitably geared to a cutter spindle, would supply all the power required, and could be used at any angle or position. A possibility which has occurred to many lathe users is the mounting of an electric drill on the lathe for milling purposes, and the only snag in this scheme is that the spindle of a light machine of this type is not usually designed to deal with side thrust as encountered in milling operations.

The use of a separate motor, mounted in a convenient position to drive a cutter spindle in the lathe, is, however,

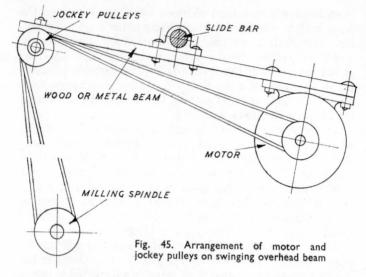

Fig. 45. Arrangement of motor and
jockey pulleys on swinging overhead beam

fairly common nowadays as a substitute for the orthodox
overhead gear, and may be found more adaptable than the
latter on certain kinds of work.   Mr. K. N. Harris uses a
driving unit comprising a baseboard on which is mounted an
electric motor, and a vertical pillar carrying a tension lever
with jockey pulleys, as shown on page 128.   The motor
is bolted to a hinged base-plate, with adjusting screws which
enable either of the three steps of the cone pulley to be aligned
with the jockey pulleys on the centre pillar.   An appliance of
this kind can be placed in any position, to suit the location of
the milling spindle, and will usually stay in place with its
own weight, or, if not, may be temporarily held by light clamps,
or a couple of screws.

Mr. F. G. Arkell uses an electric motor attached to the rear
end of a beam, similar to the tension lever of the orthodox
overhead gear, adjustable along a bar mounted over the lathe,
the motor in this case serving as a counter-weight to maintain
tension on the belt, which runs over jockey pulleys on the
front end of the beam (Fig. 45).

A rather more elaborate development of this idea is incorporated in the driving gear constructed by Messrs. F. Bontor and R. C. Marshall. In this case the beam is duplicated, and consists of two aluminium castings located some distance apart, carrying the motor mount at the rear end, and a ball-bearing countershaft at the other (Fig. 46 and page 128.) The centre housing of each beam is bored to a sliding fit on a supporting bar, which is mounted at each end in cast aluminium brackets carried by an angle-iron frame above the

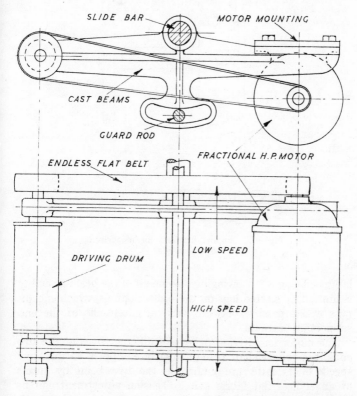

SLIDE BAR

MOTOR MOUNTING

CAST BEAMS

GUARD ROD

ENDLESS FLAT BELT

FRACTIONAL H.P. MOTOR

DRIVING DRUM

LOW SPEED

HIGH SPEED

Fig. 46. Elevation and underside plan of motorised and overhead gear

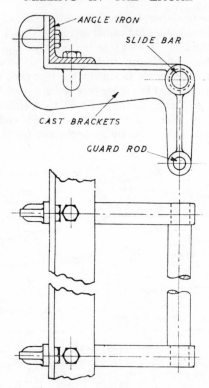

Fig. 47. Support brackets for motorised
overhead gear

lathe bed (Fig. 47). Swinging movement of the beam assembly
is limited by slotted lugs on the beam castings, which encom-
pass a bar passing between vertical extensions of the end
supporting brackets.

The motor has driving pulleys of different sizes at the two
ends, the countershaft being similarly equipped, so that two
speeds of the latter are obtainable, the drive being by means
of an endless flat fabric belt.   Tension adjustment can be
obtained by sliding the driving motor backwards or forwards.

The centre part of the countershaft is occupied by a drum or roller, which forms the drive pulley to the milling or grinding spindle mounted on the lathe slide-rest. This provides a fairly wide range of self-alignment, but a cone pulley would be equally suitable, as it is only necessary to slide the complete unit on its supporting bar to line up the drive at any position along the lathe bed.

Questions are often asked as to the power of the motor required for driving a cutter spindle in this way. This will naturally vary with the class of work being dealt with, but it may be mentioned that most of the work done in small lathes, using the appliances which have been described, can be handled with a motor of about 1/10 or $\frac{1}{8}$ h.p. Indeed, it would be found difficult to transmit more power than this by the light belt drives specified. Grinding attachments are in a different category, but here it is possible to transmit greater power by running at a higher speed.

CHAPTER VII

INDEXING GEAR

T HE need for some means of circular dividing, or " indexing," is encountered in many kinds of milling operations, but more particularly in gearcutting, and the production of polygonal or other regular geometric forms. The term " indexing " has been used here to define divisions of a circle, because " dividing " is a much broader term, embracing not only circular dividing, but also linear spacing, as on a scale or graduated ruler. However, the two terms are used more or less indiscriminately to describe the class of appliance now under discussion, and the terms " dividing head " or " dividing attachment " nearly always apply to such an appliance, though the old term " dividing engine " may mean something quite different.

It has already been shown that milling can be carried out in the lathe, either by utilising the lathe mandrel as a cutter spindle or by using an independent cutter spindle. When indexing gear is used, it must obviously be applied to the work-holding fixture in either case ; that is to say, the former method calls for an indexing appliance fitted to the slide-rest of the lathe, and the latter, for some means of indexing the lathe mandrel itself. It will, perhaps, be appropriate to describe devices applied to the latter purpose first, because they are probably the more common, and are applicable to almost any lathe, with the minimum amount of trouble in fitting up ; moreover, they can be employed for many other purposes besides milling.

The "divided headstock" fitted to many instrument, horological and ornamental lathes is perhaps the best known. As seen in Fig. 48 and on page 108, it consists of a normal type of headstock, having the large step of the driving pulley drilled on the side or rim with one or more concentric circles of equally-spaced holes, and provided with a locking pin or detent attached to the fixed part of the headstock. In most cases, the number of holes in the circle, or circles, is designed to furnish multiples of the most commonly-used divisions.

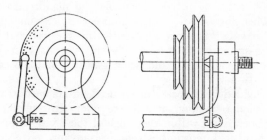

Fig. 48. The form of divided headstock once common on instrument and ornamental lathes

Thus, a circle of 60 holes will provide multiples of 2, 3, 4, 5, 6, 10, 12, 15, 20 and 30 divisions, which cover a wide range of general requirements, and is perhaps the most useful number to choose if one is limited to a single row of holes.

The locking pin in the example shown is mounted on a fairly stiff flat spring, attached at the lower end to a pillar screwed into the base of the headstock, so that the pin springs into the holes, and it is tapered to prevent backlash when in engagement. It is important also that the lower end of the spring should be firmly located so that it cannot move up or down. In some cases, a micrometer adjustment has been provided on the spring anchorage, so that it can be moved up or down by a definite amount, thus providing a "differential" adjustment, which enables divisions other than those covered by the number of holes, in the particular circle used,

to be obtained.   Generally speaking, however, an adjustment
of this nature is difficult to use correctly, and may prove to
be more trouble than it is worth.

In many lathes, the spring blade is replaced by a plunger
which slides in a hole in the headstock pillar, and is sometimes
provided with a spring, but more often is just a push-fit.
This provides greater rigidity than the spring blade, but demands very careful fitting of the pin to avoid backlash.   When
any form of spring is used, some means of holding the pin out
of action must be fitted, to enable the mandrel to rotate
freely when normal lathe work is in progress.   Spring plungers
usually have a " bayonet " catch for this purpose, but in the
case of a spring blade, it is usually only necessary to slacken
the bolt at the lower end, and swing it away from the headstock
pulley.

The divided headstock can be used, in connection with a
rotary-spindle milling attachment, for gear-cutting and
similar operations, within the range of the divisions provided
on the headstock pulley, but is at a disadvantage if some odd
number of divisions is required.   A much wider choice of
divisions is possible by fitting a dividing appliance at the tail
end of the mandrel, on which division plates or other available
means of indexing may be fitted.   In the case of screw-
cutting lathes, any of the change wheels provided with the
lathe may be used, or it is possible to mount any gear wheel
or notched plate which may be obtained to suit the particular
job in hand.

It may be found difficult or impracticable to fit the dividing
appliance on the tail end of the spindle owing to lack of space,
or the presence of casings or other fittings over the end of the
mandrel.   Some of the older lathes are fitted with a thrust
bearing on the end face of the mandrel which precludes any
such fitting.   But, in many cases, the problem may be solved by
making a temporary extension to the mandrel, in the form of
an expanding plug to fit the mandrel bore, and having a
seating to carry the gear wheel beyond the end of the mandrel,
as illustrated in Fig. 49 and on page 90.

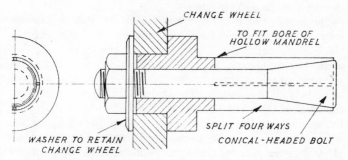

Fig. 49. Expanding plug mandrel to carry change wheels on tail end of hollow lathe mandrel

Indirect fitting of the division plate, through a geared shaft, such as the tumbler reverse gear shaft, is not desirable, because of the inevitable backlash in the gearing ; but some workers have reported success with this method if great care is taken to take up play always in the same direction.

When using a gear wheel as a division plate, the form of locking pin used with a holed plate is not usually suitable, though a pin shaped at the end to fit exactly between the teeth of the wheel can be used for light work. A better method is to use a plunger or detent having a broad bearing which will resist torque more effectively. Lathes having the usual slotted lug for the reversing pinion on the headstock casting, or a change-wheel quadrant with sufficient range to carry a locking device more or less level with the mandrel centre, may be fitted with the simple spring plunger shown in Fig. 50, the arrangement and use of which call for no explanation. Another very simple locking device, which may be fitted in much the same position, is the eccentric disc illustrated in Fig. 51. The edge of the disc is turned to fit the space between the teeth of the change wheels ; it is mounted on the square stud fitted to the quadrant or bracket, being simply pushed in to engage with the wheel teeth, and locked in position with the thumb screw.

Worm Dividing Appliances

The range of divisions obtainable from any indexing device may be enormously extended by the use of worm gearing, the increase being equal to the ratio of the worm reduction used. It is quite possible to use an ordinary spur gear, such as a change wheel, as a worm wheel, by screw-cutting a worm of suitable pitch to engage with it, as shown in Fig 52. If possible, the shaft of the worm should be placed at such an angle that the worm tooth lies normal to the tooth of the change wheel when engaged, i.e., the worm shaft centre line should be at 90 degrees, plus or minus the pitch angle of the worm, to the mandrel axis. But this is not an absolutely essential condition to accurate dividing, as the object in this case is not mechanical efficiency or good wearing properties, but simply " wedge contact " between the tooth faces.

A worm gear can be adjusted to work with no backlash whatever, and this is essential when using the worm for dividing. In some cases the worm shaft is spring-mounted,

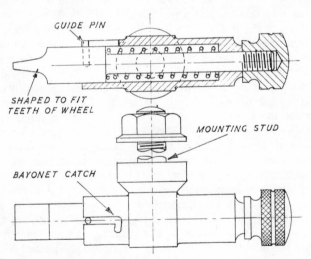

Fig. 50. Simple indexing spring plunger for use with lathe change wheels

Drummond 3½-in. " M " type bench lathe, with dividing attachment cutter spindle, and overhead gear in position

Cutter spindle driven by plastic belting from a motor mounted on lathe bed

Motorised overhead gear, by Messrs. Bontor and Marshall

so that it is held firmly up against the worm wheel ; apart from taking up play, this has the advantage of providing a quick-release movement, to allow of shifting the mandrel instantaneously when a large angle of rotation is required.

If a special worm wheel is used for the dividing appliance, the most convenient number of teeth is 60, but other numbers of teeth are often used, and, obviously, much depends upon the range of divisions obtainable at the worm shaft. The lathe change wheels may be used here also, but it is often found more convenient to fit a standard division plate, with a number of rows of holes, to give as wide a range of divisions as possible. Further refinements are the fitting of sector fingers to the division plate, to simplify counting of holes, and a thrust adjustment to eliminate any possible error through end play of the worm shaft.

It is sometimes possible to arrange worm dividing gear to engage with the large spur gear on the mandrel of a back-geared lathe, if the gear has a suitable number of teeth. This was done very neatly in the case of the Drummond 3½-in. lathe milling equipment, the worm shaft being carried in a bracket which could be mounted on the headstock casting

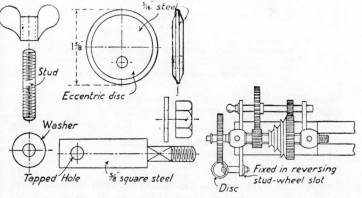

Fig. 51. Simple eccentric wedge disc indexing device

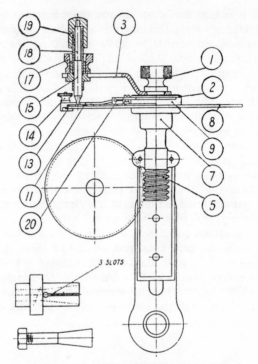

Fig. 52. Worm dividing gear as constructed by Mr. Ian Bradley

(1) Wormshaft hand nut, (2) sector plate, (3) index arm, (5) worm, (7) wormshaft bearing, (8) division plate, (9) clamping washer, (11) sector finger, (13) sector clamp, (14) clamp nut, (17) plunger housing, (18) plunger, (19) plunger knob, (20) sector joint. Expanding plug mandrel for change wheels also shown

when required. Plain indexing has also been applied to the spur wheel, a notable example being that on the Eta lathe, in which the gear wheel had 60 teeth, but was made capable of providing 120 divisions by the ingenious device of using a plunger in which the engaging end was offset to the extent of $\frac{1}{4}$ the circumferential pitch. By turning the plunger through half a revolution, the spaces between the gear teeth could be split, and the range of divisions thereby doubled.

Worm indexing gear as fitted by the writer to a Myford ML4 lathe

The Westbury dividing attachment

The Poyser Universal milling and dividing attachment

Accuracy of Indexing Gear

When indexing is carried out by dividing gear on the lathe mandrel, using a plain locking pin or detent, the accuracy of the finished work will depend on that of the division plate, assuming that backlash, spring or inadvertent movement of either the spindle or the lathe slides can be eliminated. The latter is the more difficult condition to ensure in practice. It is advisable to lock or clamp any movements not in use, and if the mandrel can be locked by any means which do not affect its rotational location, it is advisable to make use of this each time after setting the dividing gear, releasing it for shifting the mandrel. Side pressure exerted on the work during the cut may sometimes spring the locking pin out of its true position, or even force it out of engagement, unless this precaution is observed.

With worm indexing gear, the most important component in respect of accuracy is the worm wheel. Small errors in the spacing of holes or teeth in the division plate are of minor importance, as the effect of such errors is divided by the ratio of the worm reduction. It is thus possible to use improvised plates on a worm dividing appliance, and success has been obtained by using a plate spaced out with the aid of dividers for an emergency operation involving an odd number of divisions.

It may be mentioned that in most of the work encountered by the amateur, the use of the lathe change wheels gives sufficiently accurate results, either for direct or worm indexing. In gear wheels generated by a hobbing process, errors are usually very small, as the method employed tends to even them out around the wheel ; but some check on the accuracy of any device used for indexing is always advisable, if means are available for carrying it out. Specially made and tested division plates or worm wheels, however, are very expensive, and may be regarded as beyond the means of the amateur ; they are only necessary for highly exacting work, such as optical or other scientific instruments.

Making Division Plates

Many amateurs have attempted, with more or less success, to make their own division plates, and methods of doing so have often been described in *The Model Engineer*. These methods need not be discussed in detail, but it may be mentioned that one of the best-known methods of generating a division plate by first principles is to drill a number of holes in a strip of metal, using a simple drilling jig to ensure equal spacing, as shown in Fig. 53, and bend the strip into a circle embracing the required number of holes. Join the ends, fitting a dowel or rivet to align the holes, and then turn a wood or metal disc to such a diameter that the ring will just fit tightly over it, but without stretching or straining the joint. The distance between any two holes will then represent a definite and equal fraction of the circle. This method is applicable to any number of divisions, and may be found useful when some unusual number is required.

When an accurate division plate or gear wheel is available to serve as a " master," it may be copied by means of a drilling spindle in the lathe. Play in the bearings of the spindle must be eliminated, or at least reduced to an imperceptible minimum, and a short, stiff drill employed, a small centre-drill being recommended, if the depth of hole is not too great. On no account should a division plate be copied by clamping it against the blank plate and drilling through the holes.

The " back-to-back " method of copying a division plate is recommended, however, in conjunction with a drilling spindle in the lathe. In this case, the master plate and the blank are mounted together, though not necessarily in contact, on a true-running mandrel between the lathe centres. A locking pin is mounted in a convenient position on the lathe bed to engage the holes in the master plate, the drilling spindle being mounted on the slide-rest, and used on the blank as each hole in the master plate is located and engaged. This method has the advantage of providing a sensitive " feel," by eliminating the friction of the lathe mandrel bearings, or other additional fittings which may be involved in fitting up more complex indexing gear.

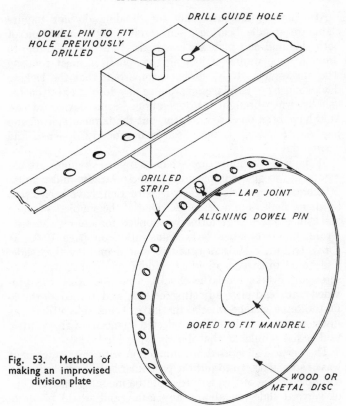

DRILL GUIDE HOLE

DOWEL PIN TO FIT
HOLE PREVIOUSLY
DRILLED

DRILLED
STRIP

LAP JOINT

ALIGNING DOWEL PIN

BORED TO FIT MANDREL

Fig. 53. Method of
making an improvised
division plate

WOOD OR
METAL DISC

In the class of dividing attachments intended for use on the lathe slide-rest, the principles employed are similar to those of the lathe headstock dividing appliances, but in addition, they embody extra features to facilitate mounting and (in some cases) vertical adjustment, also means for mounting work between centres or in a collet chuck. The function of a rotary-spindle milling attachment is often combined with that of a dividing attachment, by the provision of division-plates, either to mount direct on the spindle, or for use in conjunction with worm reduction gearing.

Attachments designed only for dividing do not require elaborate spindle bearings, but rigidity and elimination of both side and end play are essential. It is also desirable to provide some means of locking the spindle against rotation when necessary. It is, however, important that the locking device must not displace or produce any torque effect on the spindle, when brought into operation. Some devices of this kind have been open to criticism, but the familiar split clamp method of locking is fairly sound if properly designed and carried out.

Many lathe manufacturers have supplied dividing attachments as special equipment for their lathes, and similar attachments, or parts for their construction, have been listed by many makers of accessories. One of the simplest of these attachments was that formerly supplied for use on the 4-in. Drummond round-bed lathe (illustration on page 107). It consisted of a casting designed to mount on a vertical slide, and bored to carry a dividing spindle, one end of which was screwcut to take the lathe chucks, while the other was provided with end-play adjusting collars, and turned down to fit the lathe change-wheels, the latter being thus utilised as division-plates. Indexing was effected by means of an eccentric wedge disc, similar to that illustrated in Fig. 51.

The vertical slide used in conjunction with this attachment was of special design to suit the particular lathe, but obviously, a simple device of this nature could be mounted on any type of vertical slide, on almost any lathe, and would be quite suitable for producing small spur or bevel gears to a sufficiently high degree of accuracy for most practical purposes. Work of this kind is often regarded as a *bête noire* by model engineers, but it is by no means as formidable as it looks, and excellent gears have been cut with the aid of equipment far more primitive than that illustrated here.

The facility for using the lathe chucks on the spindle of the dividing attachment is extremely useful, as apart from saving the expense or complication of extra chucks, it enables a chuck to be transferred from the lathe mandrel nose with work *in situ*, and concentric accuracy thereby to be ensured in the milling operation. In most small lathes, however, the room available on the slide-rest is rather inadequate to accommodate large chucks, and their overhang is also rather excessive for a light dividing spindle. The use of chucks or other work-holding fixtures specially designed to suit the spindle is therefore highly desirable.

Some designers of these appliances, in their desire to promote rigidity, and the ability to handle large or heavy work, have succeeded in achieving only clumsiness and restricted movement, and it is often found that a light appliance, with limited capacity, is much handier to use, and of more practical utility.

The " Westbury " Dividing Attachment

An interesting light dividing attachment was described in *The Model Engineer* over twenty years ago by the author. This device, Fig. 54, and page 130, embodied two headstocks mounted on a round bar, one of which carried the dividing spindle, with its indexing gear, while the other carried a double-ended sliding back centre. In its original form, indexing was effected by division-plates mounted directly on the spindle, in conjunction either with a fixed detent, or a fixed division-plate and dowel-pin, which enabled a multiplication of divisions to be obtained on the vernier principle. A worm dividing gear was, however, found to be much handier, the worm wheel having 60 teeth and the worm shaft being mounted in a bracket adjustable around the headstock, so that it could be located in the most convenient position for operating.

The really novel feature of this appliance, however, was the method of mounting it in the lathe, which provided a universal latitude of angular adjustment, and made it possible to dispense with the use of a vertical slide for height adjustment. This was effected by mounting the slide bar in a cross hole drilled through the head of a tapered bolt, the latter being split on the centre line of the cross hole, so as to act as a split collet when drawn into a tapered hole in the shank. In this way, the slide bar was firmly gripped, and the rotational movement of the bolt simultaneously locked, by the tightening of a single nut. With the shank held in the lathe tool-post, the dividing centres could be brought into the required angle and position for operating on either spur, bevel, worm or skew gears as required.

Small diameter division plates, with a single row of holes, were used with this device, to simplify operation and avoid taking up too much room. The plates could be produced in a few minutes by copying from the lathe change-wheels, with the aid of a drilling spindle. Despite the small size and lightness of the appliance, it could be used to cut involute spur gears in steel up to 2-in. diameter, using home-made cutters, or clock gears in brass up to 3-in. diameter, using fly-cutters. The blanks were mounted either on mandrels between male or female centres, or on tapered arbors to fit the socket of the live spindle, with or without the support of the back centre.

The " Quickset " Dividing Attachment

Another interesting light appliance of this nature is produced by the Quickset Tool Holder Co., of Stanmore, Middlesex, the dividing centres being in this case mounted in fixed headstocks in a single casting, which constitutes the frame or bed, and is intended to be mounted on a vertical slide. This is obviously a more rigid device than the previous one, but rather less versatile ·in scope, though it will deal with a wide range of gear cutting, tap or reamer fluting, and similar work.

The worm wheel in this case has 90 teeth, and three division plates, each having three rows of holes, are supplied with the complete attachment. Locking clamps are provided on both the spindle headstock and the supporting centre, and the spindle nose is bored to take standard collets (page 133).

The " Eureka " Milling Attachment

Mr. J. B. S. Poyser, of Peck's Hill, Mansfield, Notts, has introduced many ingenious lathe attachments and other appliances in the past, and the " Eureka " Universal Milling

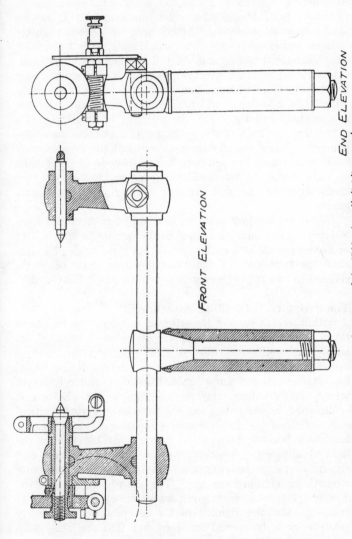

END ELEVATION

FRONT ELEVATION

Fig. 54. Front and end elevations of the "Westbury" dividing attachment

Attachment illustrated on page 130, is one of his contributions to the range of devices now under consideration. It can be used either as a dividing attachment or a rotary cutter spindle, and embodies its own vertical slide, with a rotatable base, graduated throughout the full 360 degrees. The headstock bracket is mounted on the vertical slide, and is bored with two parallel holes, of equal size, one of which carries a tubular " quill " or housing in which the complete spindle assembly is mounted, and the other the overarm or steady bar for supporting the back centre. The position of these two components is therefore interchangeable to suit the type of work being handled, and in addition, it is possible to fit the spindle at right-angles to the headstock, by making use of the combination bracket and bar seen to the right of the photograph.

The worm dividing gear can be completely detached from the quill, and a pulley attached to the spindle to enable it to be driven for use as a cutter spindle. A wide range of adaptability is thus afforded, and the appliance may be justly claimed to live up to the much-abused title of " Universal."

The " Myford " Dividing Attachment

Within recent years, the Myford Engineering Co. have taken a very serious interest in the provision of attachments for increasing the versatility of their popular lathes, and in keeping with the general policy in the design of the latter, the attachments are simple, robust and comparatively low in price. The dividing attachment shown in the photograph is designed for mounting on the standard Myford vertical slide, either of the fixed or swivelling type. It comprises a headstock bracket, adapted to bolt against the face of the slide at any angle, which carries the dividing spindle and also the overarm, the latter being tubular to provide maximum strength in relation to weight. The worm gearing, with the division plates supplied, gives an extremely wide range of divisions, and the rigidity of the assembly enables fairly heavy work to be carried out, providing that the lathe slides are in good order and correctly adjusted.

When cutting spur gears with an attachment of this type, it is usual to set the blank mandrel above and at right-angles to the lathe axis, lowering the vertical slide to adjust depth of cut, and traversing by means of the cross-slide from front to back, i.e. against the cutter rotation. With some of the smaller dividing appliances, it is possible to work with the blank below the cutter, which enables the progress of the work to be better observed ; in this case the traverse should be from back to front, with normal direction of lathe rotation. Sometimes it is possible to arrange the arbor axis vertically, in which case the feed is applied by the cross-slide, and traverse by the vertical slide, upwards if at the front of the cutter, and downwards if at the rear.

Skew gears—not true helical gears, but spur gears with teeth at a slight angle to promote quiet running—may be produced by swivelling the base of the vertical slide to the required angle, and working with the arbor horizontal. Worm gears may be " gashed " to about three-quarters of the tooth depth by arranging the attachment in the same way, but in this case the arbor is only fed vertically in the exact centre of the blank, and not traversed. Worm gears should always be finished by hobbing with a cutter of the same pitch and diameter as the mating worm, the relative angles of the work and hob spindles being the same as that of the worm and wheel ; that is, usually at right-angles, though occasionally worm gearing is used for transmission at other angles. Worm gears cannot be generated, neither can true helical gears be cut, by simple attachments of this type, as some means of rotating the dividing spindle in relation to traversing movement is necessary for this class of work, but it is by no means impossible to devise attachments which will perform this work. In universal milling machines, the dividing head is geared to the traversing spindle of the machine table by means of change gears, to produce spiral motion ; and the same principle has been successfully applied to milling in the lathe.

For cutting bevel gears, the work arbor can be set at an angle in front of the cutter, and the feed applied by the cross-slide, with vertical traversing movement in an upward direction. In most cases, it is impossible to support the bevel gear blank between centres, as the extended mandrel would foul the cutter ; it is, therefore necessary to use a socketed arbor or a collet chuck. Bevel gears having truly radial teeth can only be generated by a shaping process, but a sufficiently accurate approximation for most purposes may be produced by milling, if a cutter narrower than the finished tooth space is used, and side cuts subsequently taken to produce equal taper of teeth and tooth spaces. It will be apparent that a single " forming " cut taken with a gear cutter will produce a parallel tooth space, and an excessively tapered tooth. Two gears cut in this way would make contact only on the outside radial edges of the teeth, and could not possibly mate together sweetly.

Gears should always be cut in accordance with the formulae provided in reference tables of standard gearing, using cutters of the correct form, and feeding to the correct depth. Blank diameters are also highly important ; the use of a micrometer is advised in machining gear blanks, and an index graduated in thousandths of an inch, on the feed screw of the attachment, will be found extremely useful in assessing the depth of the cut. But gearcutting is not nearly so formidable an operation as it is often believed to be, and there are few amateurs who have tackled it in a determined manner who have failed to produce satisfactory results.

CHAPTER VIII

APPLICATION OF LATHE MILLING
PROCESSES

NUMEROUS examples have already been given of the kind of milling operations which are frequently encountered in model engineering, and how they may be carried out in the lathe by the various methods and appliances described. The purpose of this chapter is mainly to give general advice to the reader as to the scope and possibilities of lathe milling processes, and how they may best be applied to the problems he encounters in the construction of particular types of models.

The order in which the methods and appliances have been described may be taken as indicating the order of their complexity, and also of the skill and experience required to employ them to the best advantage. If one attempts to use an elaborate milling attachment right away, with no experience of the simpler methods, it is as likely as not that an unfavourable impression will be obtained. In order to exploit any machine or process effectively, it is just as important to know what it will not do as what it will do.

Many of the disappointments which have resulted from attempts to carry out milling in the lathe have been due to attempting too large a job, either in respect of its actual size, or in the extent of the cutting operation. It was pointed out at the beginning of this book that the lathe cannot be regarded as an efficient milling machine from the point of view of its ability to take heavy cuts and remove large amounts of metal. But even when the actual cut is light, the size of the workpiece itself often has an important influence on the success of the operation. A large casting or other structural part may not only be unwieldy, and completely dwarf the slide to which it is attached, but the distance of the surface to be operated on from the actual point of support may be excessive, so that undue leverage is exerted on the slides, and the liability to spring or chatter is much increased.

Wherever possible, large pieces should be bolted directly to the cross-slide, with solid packing pieces and secure clamping devices, and operated on by a milling cutter in the lathe chuck. If, however, vertical adjustment becomes necessary, and a vertical slide must be used, the limitations of the method soon become apparent. To take a common example, attempts are often made to mill out the slots to take the hornblocks in locomotive frames in a small lathe, generally with indifferent results. The method usually employed is to bolt the pair of frames together and hold them horizontally in a machine vice attached to the vertical slide, using an end mill in the lathe chuck to form the slot. In this case there is usually a considerable amount of spring in the work itself, apart from that of the slides, and the result is only too often bad chattering, snatching and digging in of the cutter.

An alternative method of dealing with this kind of operation is to clamp it longitudinally, in a horizontal position, over the cross-slide, at approxmately centre height, and use either a double side and face cutter, or a fly-cutter, mounted in the centre of a long mandrel. This method certainly provides much greater rigidity, but it calls for a lathe having a clear length of bed at least twice as long as the distance between the end slots of the frames, which is generally out of the question, so far as the equipment of the average model constructor is concerned. One may conclude, therefore, that this particular job is one that does not lend itself well to a milling process, and the more common and humbler method of filing out the slots will generally be found more satisfactory.

To jump to the conclusion that only a very large or heavy lathe is suitable for adaptation for milling, however, is quite erroneous, because even the lightest lathes have been applied with great success to milling operations within their capacity. Another fallacy which is often entertained is that milling in the lathe requires more power than normal lathe work. The fact is that an attempt to use the full power available on the average lathe would be more likely to strain the slides and bearings than to effect any useful purpose. A fairly high torque at low speed is sometimes very useful in milling operations, just as it is in heavy turning operations, but so far as cutting rate is concerned, attempts to force the pace generally defeat their own purpose.

The beginner often fails to realise the side stress imposed in milling operations, and attempts to take too deep a cut or put on too heavy a feed. Overloading of cutters, with rapid dulling of the cutting edge, or breakage of teeth, is very common. Trouble is often caused by snatching of the cutter, due to insufficiently tight adjustment of slides, or feeding in the wrong direction.

Most model engineers will find that the small "finicky" operations provide the best scope for milling in the lathe. Many jobs which would call for tedious and skilful hand filing or fitting can be carried out very quickly by milling, often with the simplest appliances, or practically none at all. For instance, a slotted fork joint on a link or connecting-rod can be milled out by clamping the work in the lathe tool-post, and using a slotting cutter or thick slitting saw (Fig. 55). The end of the fork may be rounded off neatly, and concentric with the pivot pin, by a simple milling process.

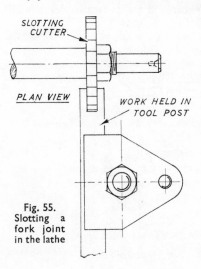

SLOTTING CUTTER

PLAN VIEW

WORK HELD IN TOOL POST

Fig. 55.
Slotting a fork joint in the lathe

A support bar, fitted with a vertical pin fitting the cross hole in the fork is mounted in the tool-post at such a height that the work is roughly symmetrical about centre level. By feeding the work up to a suitable end or face mill, and working the forked rod round the pin, a perfect semi-circle can be milled on the end (Fig. 56). An alternative arrangement consists of mounting the work on a horizontal pivot, and using a side mill (or an end mill with side teeth). This is more convenient for some classes of work, but needs firm control of the work to avoid snatching (Fig. 57).

Model steam engines of all kinds entail in their construction many operations which can be carried out by milling. Motion work, including rods, links, levers and crossheads, also slide-valve and joint faces on cylinders and steam chests, all offer scope in this direction. The cavity of a slide-valve can be produced more readily by milling than by any other process. Small boiler fittings, including check-valves, gauge-glass mountings, injectors, and feed pumps can offer many outlets for skill and initiative in the application of milling processes.

In the construction of historic types of engines, in which one of the most salient features is the beautiful detail work

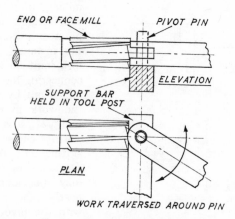

Fig. 56. Rounding the end of fork

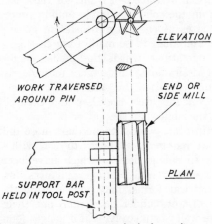

ELEVATION

WORK TRAVERSED
AROUND PIN

END OR
SIDE MILL

PLAN

SUPPORT BAR
HELD IN TOOL POST

Fig. 57. An alternative method of rounding end
of fork

in the structural parts, it is often difficult to obtain small
castings sufficiently accurate and clean to do adequate justice
to the prototype. It is not only practicable, but often well
worth while, to devise means of milling these parts.   The
constructor of a very remarkable set of beam pumping engines
produced the fluted columns of the entablature by milling,
and pedestals, brackets and panels, with geometric designs
either in relief or intaglio, have also been machined by similar
means.

Axle-boxes for model locomotives are often milled on the
sides to provide accurate sliding surfaces to work in the hornblocks. Saddle fittings for chimney, dome and safety-valve,
which have to fit accurately on the rounded top of the boiler,
may be milled to the exact radius required by means of an
adjustable fly-cutter ;   the same method may be used in
machining a cast smokebox saddle. The base of a traction
engine cylinder presents a very similar machining problem,
which can be disposed of in exactly the same way.

The milling of cams, which is necessary in constructing
many kinds of machines, and model petrol engines in particular,

has already been described. Pistons for these engines can be machined from the solid by simple milling processes, and in the smaller sizes of engines at least, are generally sounder and often lighter than those made from castings. The many toolmaking operations which the model engineer finds it necessary or desirable to undertake, may nearly always be facilitated or expedited by the judicious use of milling processes. Not the least useful of the capabilities in this direction is the ability of the cutter to " propagate its own species," or in other words, to produce more milling cutters when they are required in a hurry to deal with special jobs.

The many ingenious devices which have been developed by makers of ornamental turning appliances, for cutting intricate geometrical forms, may not be directly applicable to the class of work under discussion, but their underlying principles are well worth studying if it is ever found necessary to tackle some milling operation of unusual complexity. It is also noteworthy that these appliances were used for working on all sorts of materials, including metals, wood, ivory, bone and even mineral substances such as marble and other stone. This is a reminder that milling can be usefully applied to the woodworking department of the model workshop, and is an extremely valuable aid in patternmaking or in making small " cabinet " parts for models. The wood-workers' tenoning machines, routers, chain mortisers, and spindle moulders are all specialised forms of milling machines.

Mr. E. W. Fraser has furnished some particulars of a very useful vertical slide of his own design and construction, which is in regular use on his 5-in. I.X.L. lathe. This is of particularly sturdy and rigid design, and its special feature is the combination machine vice built into the sliding member. Mr. Fraser states that this fitting is practically a permanent attachment to the rear end of the lathe cross-slide, and when not required for milling, it can be used to hold a rear parting or forming tool. As may be seen from Fig. 58, the slide is of the non-swivelling type, the traversing slideway being integral with the mounting bracket, which consists of a heavy angle-plate with two bracing ribs or struts. The sliding member is

The " Quickset " dividing attachment

Cutting a bevel gear with the " Myford " dividing attachment

Two views of the " Myford " dividing attachment

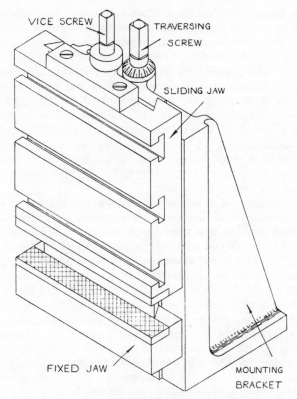

Fig. 58. Mr. E.W. Fraser's combined vertical slide and machine vice

fitted with a subsidiary slide, having tee slots in its front surface, and forming the moving jaw of a parallel vice. Both this and the stationary jaw on the lower end of the main slide are equipped with hardened steel inserts.

Cutting Feeds and Speeds

It is beyond all question that these are most important matters, and indeed essential to success in all machine tool operations ; but the idea so often entertained that complete data on this subject can be compiled in the form of a simple table, taking into account only materials, tool steels and surface speeds, is quite fallacious. The nature of the milling operation affects cutting speed very considerably, just as in lathe work, parting, forming and screwcutting operations nearly always demand a reduction of speed, compared to that used for ordinary turning. Similarly, it is often found necessary to reduce speed if the cutter has a tendency to chatter. A machine having a really rigid spindle and slides can safely be run at a much higher speed than one of lighter design, and this fact accounts very largely for the high speeds used in modern production milling.

For milling in small lathes, it will generally be found advisable to use substantially lower speeds, for a given type of work and cutter, than those used in milling machine practice. Small end mills may be run at the top speed of the lathe, and fly-cutters, when used on brass or softer materials, generally work best at the higher speeds. But for larger cutters, speed should always be reduced, and for side and face mills working in steel and cast-iron, it will generally be found best to use the back gear of the lathe, when cutters are used in the lathe mandrel, or a worm or spur gear reduction when a milling spindle is employed. Even in the production shop, experience is the only sound guide to the most efficient cutting speeds ; and in the home workshop, where speed of production is of secondary importance, the golden rule is " When in doubt—reduce speed ! "

To conclude, thanks are expressed to all readers of *The Model Engineer* who have contributed by furnishing hints and data, illustrations and opinions. No claim is made that this book exhausts the whole subject of milling in the lathe. But it is believed that typical examples have been given of all well-known and established types of appliances and their use, and sufficient detailed information on technique to assist the beginner to carry out simple operations, and to guide him past the worst snags and pitfalls.